101 Weekend
Cross Stitch Gifts

Lesley Teare

**Over 350 quick-to-stitch
motifs for perfect presents**

David and Charles

Dedication

To Rosemary, for walking up the garden path.

A DAVID & CHARLES BOOK
David & Charles is a subsidiary of F+W (UK) Ltd.,
an F+W Publications Inc. company

First published in the UK in 2005

Distributed in North America
by F+W Publications, Inc.
4700 East Galbraith Road
Cincinnati, OH 45236
1-800-289-0963

A catalogue record for this book is available from the British Library.

ISBN 0 7153 1945 0 hardback

Printed in Singapore by KHL Printing Co Pte Ltd
for David & Charles
Brunel House   Newton Abbot   Devon

Executive Commissioning Editor Cheryl Brown
Editor Jennifer Proverbs
Senior Art Editor Prudence Rogers
Production Controller Ros Napper
Project Editor Juliet Bracken
Photographers Karl Adamson and Simon Whitmore

Visit our website at www.davidandcharles.co.uk

David & Charles books are available from all good bookshops; alternatively you can contact our
Orderline on (0)1626 334555 or write to us at FREEPOST EX2 110, David & Charles Direct,
Newton Abbot, TQ12 4ZZ (no stamp required UK mainland).

 # contents

Introduction

It is the sentiment behind a gift that counts and a hand crafted, personalized gift is sure to be treasured. In this book you will find 101 gorgeous gift ideas to inspire you.

Whether you have a whole weekend or just an hour to spare, you will find small keepsakes to make for every occasion throughout the year. From the birth of a baby or a young child's first day at school, to a wedding, a christening and other celebration days, there are lots of fun motifs that will make the perfect last minute offering.

All the motifs are quick to stitch using the colour keys provided. They are also flexible and can be presented in many ways. You can either make your gift exactly as shown or adapt the designs according to the time you have for stitching. The bears from the padded door hanger on page 9, for example, are perfect for stitching on a baby bib. You can often repeat motifs to make a border. The boat motif in the children's section on page 14 makes a lovely towel decoration that will appeal to children and adults alike.

There are also decorative alphabets so you can easily adapt the designs to create personalized presents by adding initials, names and dates. Some alphabet designs are quite traditional, while others have a more modern feel, but they can all be used to make momentos for many different occasions. Look through each chapter for more inspiration.

In creating the designs for this book I have not only made up my own gifts but also mounted the stitched pieces in items bought from craft stores, listed on page 102. These suggestions are sure to spark off your own ideas for ways of presenting your stitching. Of course, many of the designs can also be stitched as greetings cards, so you should never be short of a quick momento made by your own fair hands.

I hope you will have a lot of fun making gifts your family and friends will treasure.

Start stitching now

If you can't wait to get started on making the designs, here is the basic stitching information you will need. For more detailed stitching and finishing instructions turn to pages 90 and 94. Most of the designs are stitched on 14-count Aida or 28-count evenweave linen and, unless otherwise stated, the following stitching principles apply.

Carefully prepare your fabric for stitching, finding and marking the centre with a stitch (see pages 90–91)

Begin in the centre on both the chart and your fabric, and work outwards across the design (see Basic Techniques page 91)

When stitching on 14-count Aida, work each cross stitch over one block of the fabric. On 28-count linen, work each cross stitch over two fabric threads. Use a size 26 tapestry needle for this (see page 91)

Use two strands of cotton for the cross stitch and one strand for the backstitch, unless otherwise stated (see page 90).

Refer to the key for which shades of stranded cotton and metallic thread to use (see page 90).

Use the alphabets to personalize your work, planning the lettering on graph paper first (see page 91).

When all the stitching is complete, carefully wash the fabric if necessary and press it face down (see page 91).

Prepare your design for framing or mounting following the making up instructions (see pages 93–101).

Babies & Children

Capture the milestones of childhood, from baby's arrival to the teen years, with this series of delightful motifs to make into gifts.

The birth of a baby is a special event that calls for a handmade keepsake. A sampler or rattle decorated with simple nursery shapes worked in soft pastel shades will be a joy for a new mother and her baby. The pretty motifs can be used to cover a photo album and make other practical and appealing gifts, too.

You'll find lots of wonderful gifts to make for a growing child – from the teddy cakeband for a first birthday cake and soft fabric cube for toddlers, to fun and funky gifts for older children. You can use the motifs to decorate all sorts of items they will love – including notebooks, pencil cases, sports bags, tee-shirts and beach towels.

Whether you're waiting for baby to arrive or looking for inspiration for a present for a teenager, you will find lots of quick motifs to make a special momento for them.

Make a special gift to welcome a new arrival or to celebrate a growing child's birthday. There are lots of gorgeous gifts for older children, too.

Welcome baby

Teddies, ducks and bunnies, in pretty pastel shades are perfect for welcoming a newborn to the world.

Design size
5 x 8cm (2 x 3¼in)
Stitch count 26 x 44

Decorate a photo album with stitched motifs as a gift for new parents to help them capture baby's early years. The pink rabbits and pretty border motif match the pink gingham album cover beautifully. Trim and fringe the edges of the stitched fabric before attaching it to a coloured backing card and sticking this to the front of the album (see page 93).

Design size
8 x 8cm (3¼ x 3¼in)
Stitch count
43 x 43

This padded door hanger is the ideal gift for the parents of a newborn to help them remind visitors to go softly. Instructions for making a padded hanging can be found on page 99. But for an even quicker gift idea, make the design into a sachet (see page 98) to hang with a pretty ribbon over the cot or cradle.

A bar of soap makes a simple yet attractive gift for a new mother. Add a ribbon and a stitched tag and it becomes rather special. I stitched the rattle motif on 14-count Aida, trimmed and stuck it on to yellow card to match the ribbon. Use pinking shears to trim your fabric and card for a pretty effect.

Design size
2.5 x 3.2cm (1 x 1¼in)
Stitch size 14 x 20

Design size
3.75 x 3.75cm
(1½ x 1½in)
Stitch count
18 x 18

Add a motif to a colourful baby's flannel to go with your soap gift. The cute duck motif with a green chequered background made the perfect decoration for a pretty yellow flannel. Trim your stitched design, leaving enough of a border to fringe and stitch the square on to the flannel (see page 100).

DMC stranded cotton

Cross stitch

I ecru	743	818	3609	• 3865
402	745	828	3806	
∕ 727	O 761	955	3819	

Backstitch

— 310
— 680
— 3607

French knots

● 310

Baby's first gifts

Here are some more cute gifts to welcome a new baby into the world.

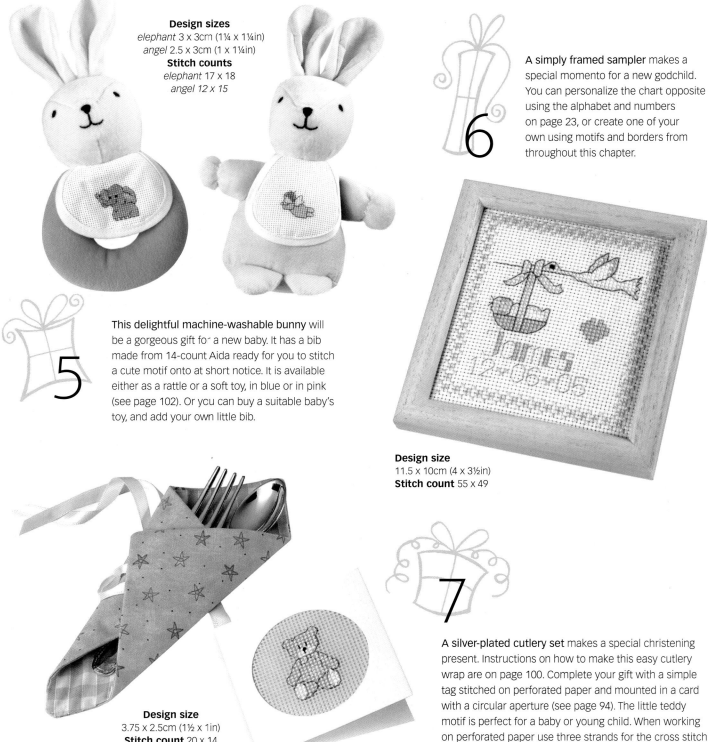

Design sizes
elephant 3 x 3cm (1¼ x 1¼in)
angel 2.5 x 3cm (1 x 1¼in)
Stitch counts
elephant 17 x 18
angel 12 x 15

A simply framed sampler makes a special momento for a new godchild. You can personalize the chart opposite using the alphabet and numbers on page 23, or create one of your own using motifs and borders from throughout this chapter.

6

5 This delightful machine-washable bunny will be a gorgeous gift for a new baby. It has a bib made from 14-count Aida ready for you to stitch a cute motif onto at short notice. It is available either as a rattle or a soft toy, in blue or in pink (see page 102). Or you can buy a suitable baby's toy, and add your own little bib.

Design size
11.5 x 10cm (4 x 3½in)
Stitch count 55 x 49

Design size
3.75 x 2.5cm (1½ x 1in)
Stitch count 20 x 14

7

A silver-plated cutlery set makes a special christening present. Instructions on how to make this easy cutlery wrap are on page 100. Complete your gift with a simple tag stitched on perforated paper and mounted in a card with a circular aperture (see page 94). The little teddy motif is perfect for a baby or young child. When working on perforated paper use three strands for the cross stitch and one strand for the backstitch (see page 91).

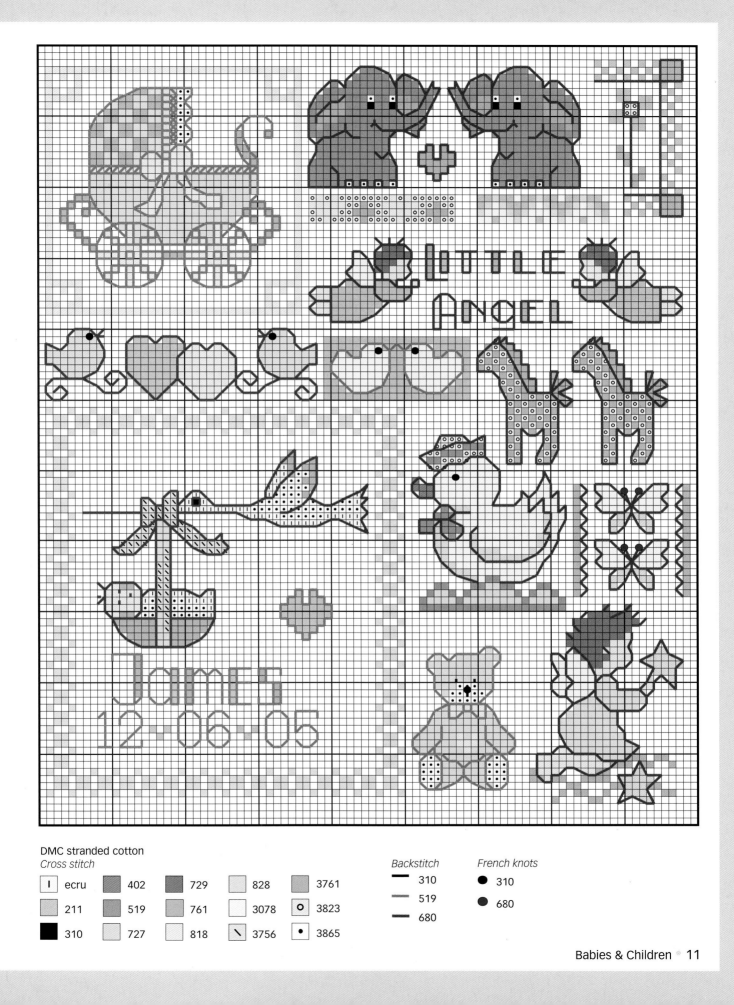

DMC stranded cotton
Cross stitch

I ecru	402	729	828	3761
211	519	761	3078	O 3823
310	727	818	\ 3756	• 3865

Backstitch
— 310
— 519
— 680

French knots
● 310
● 680

One year old

Celebrate baby's first birthday in style with these quick cards, gifts or decorations for the birthday table.

Design size *for one pattern repeat* 16.5 x 3.25cm (6½ x 1¼in) plus turnings
Stitch count 79 x 19

Design size and **stitch count** varies with each motif

8
Stitch a colourful band to go round the cake and make it the centrepiece of the table. Aida band comes in many sizes and colours (see page 97), and is usually cross stitched in three strands of cotton (see page 91). You can stitch other charted motifs on your band, for example, the two bears and hearts for a twin celebration or the teddy train for a little boy who loves trains. Use the numbers on page 23 to show a different age.

9
Small motifs make perfect gift tags for baby's first birthday. I stitched mine on perforated paper using three strands for the cross stitch and one strand for the backstitch (see page 91). I used pretty coloured card to back the stitched perforated paper and shiny ribbon to attach the finished tag to the present (see page 93).

10
Stitch your favourite motif on a pretty lemon baby's bib. This has a white 14-count Aida panel across the bottom for a design (see page 00). You can also make your own bib or attach your stitched Aida panel to the bottom of one you have bought, finishing the edges with matching binding tape. See gift 9 for how to make the tag.

Design size
7 x 4cm (2¾ x 1½in)
Stitch size
37 x 17

11
This handy sipper cup will make a delightful present for a young child (see page 102). The stitched design is inserted in a cavity in the mug to keep it clean. I stitched the train border but the teddies border or several of the smaller motifs will look just as good.

Design size
8 x 4.5cm (3¼ x 1¾in)
Stitch count 43 x 24

DMC stranded cotton
Cross stitch

I	ecru	/	676		745		826		3705		3819
	155		729	•	746		827		3713		
—	420		743		819		954		3806		

Backstitch
— 310
— 420
— 3607

French knots
● 310
● 3607

Tidy toddlers

Young children will love these bright, fun motifs when stitched on practical gifts for the home.

Design size
4.5 x 4.5cm (1¾ x 1¾in)
Stitch count 24 x 25

12 This pretty gingham hanger will encourage a little girl to hang up her clothes. It comes with a small Aida heart ready for you to stitch a design on (see page 102). You can also decorate your own hanger by stitching your motif on plastic canvas (see page 91), trimming this to shape, and attaching it as a durable tag.

13 Make a fun, quick gift to help a young child find their boots easily. The stitched motifs are attached to clips used for keeping small wellingtons together. You can buy a kit containing the vinylweave canvas and clips you need (see page 102). You can make your own clips by stitching the motif on plastic canvas, cutting it to size and gluing it to plastic pegs.

Design size *boot motif 2.5cm x 2.5cm (1 x 1in); shoe motif 3 x 2cm (1¼ x ¾in)*
Stitch count *boot motif 13 x12; shoe motif 15 x 11*

14

Make bathtime more fun for a toddler by stitching a bright border for their towel. Stitch a line of your favourite motifs along some Aida band before sewing this in place on the towel (see page 97). I used a band with a decorative edge to match the towel.

Design size 6.5 x 4.5cm (2½ x 1¾in)
Stitch count 32 x 24

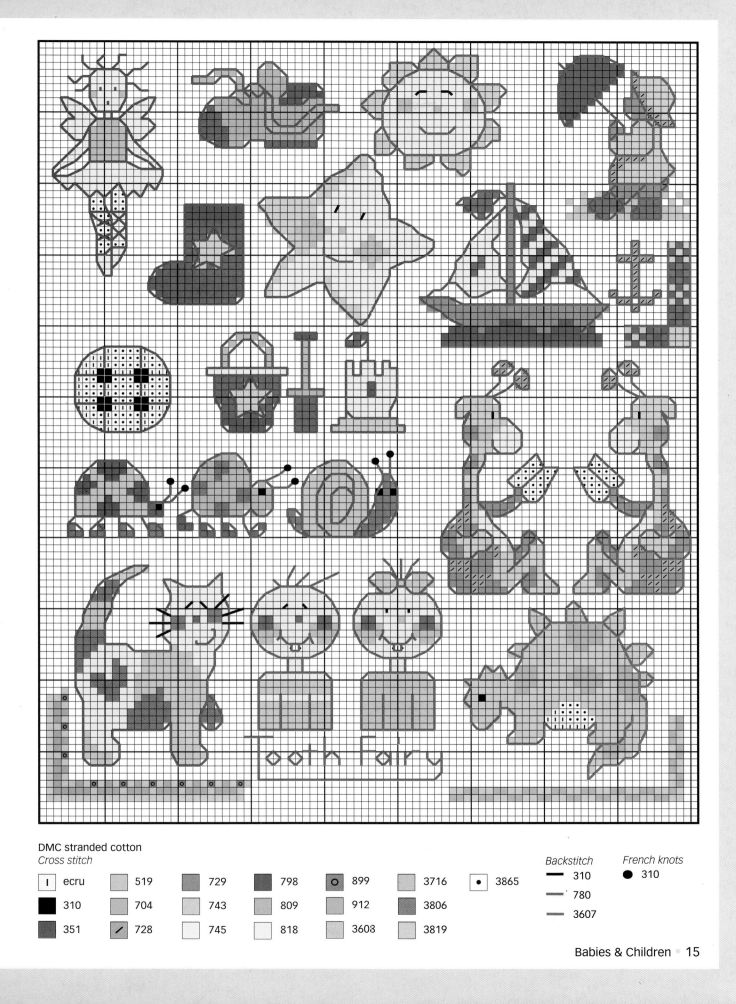

DMC stranded cotton
Cross stitch

I ecru	519	729	798	○ 899	3716	• 3865		
310	704	743	809	912	3806			
351	╱ 728	745	818	3608	3819			

Backstitch
— 310
— 780
— 3607

French knots
● 310

Favourite pastimes

Make a set of accessories that are fun and practical, inspired by children's different hobbies and sports.

15

This pretty bag is just what a little girl needs to keep her ballet shoes in. The design is stitched on Aida band and instructions on how to make the bag are on page 96. You can also make a bag for a boy to keep his football boots or gym kit in. These motifs are ideal for adding to clothing or edging a child's pillow case.

Design size *girl's bag* 5 x 3.5cm (2 x 1½in); *boy's bag* 3.5 x 4.5cm (1½ x 1¾in)
Stitch count *girl's bag* 29 x 20; *boy's bag* 22 x 24

16

Personalize a child's cap you have bought with a fun badge stitched on plastic canvas. I trimmed the canvas around the edge of the design (see pages 91 and 93) and attached it to the cap with velcro.

Design size: *star* 5 x 4.5cm (2 x 1¾in); *rosette* 3.75 x 4.2cm (1½ x 1¾in)
Stitch count: *star* 26 x 24; *rosette* 22 x24

DMC stranded cotton

Cross stitch

• blanc	◦ 310	422	728	798	822
ecru	347	433	744	— 801	961
╱ 167	350	605	797	819	3852

Backstitch
— 310
— 433

Cool kids

These fun designs are perfect for transforming notebooks and other stationery items into special gifts.

Design size *lips*, 3.75 x 2cm (1½ x ¾in); *lipstick* 1.5 x 5cm (½ x 2in) **Stitch count** *lips* 20 x 10; *lipstick* 6 x 26

Design size
girl 3 x 9cm (1¼ x 3½in)
boy 3.75 x 9cm (1½ x 3½in)
Stitch count
girl 15 x 49
boy 20 x 48

17

Here's a stylish way to present a gift to a teenager. Conceal it in a box you have decorated with one of these fun motifs stitched on perforated paper (see page 91 and 93). The boxes can be used afterwards for storing jewellery and other items.

18

Everyone likes a notebook – especially one personalized with these cool characters on the cover. You can either attach your stitched motif to a notebook you have bought (see page 93), or make it into a handy bookmark using perforated paper and a ribbon instead.

19

Design size *with seven segments* 2.5 x 15.3cm (1 x 6in) **Stitch count** 13 x 82

Children will love this quirky caterpillar ruler. The design is stitched on perforated paper and mounted in a perspex ruler (see page 102). You can add your child's name using the lower case alphabet on page 23 and vary the number of segments on your caterpillar as required.

20

Brighten up an ordinary fabric or plastic pencil case using these motifs as a fun gift for a schoolbag. Draw as many pencils as you wish, and use the alphabet on page 23 if you prefer to stitch a child's name. Trim and fringe the edges of your stitched fabric before sticking it in place on the pencil case (see page 101) .

Design size 5.5 x 4.5cm (2¼ x 1¾in) **Stitch count** 30 x 24

DMC stranded cotton
Cross stitch

• blanc	◎ 422	728	799	3607	3819	
╱ 155	680	744	819	3608		
347	704	798	3072	3801		

Backstitch
— 975
— 3607

Easy as ABC

These nursery alphabets are ideal for making personalized gifts for a baby or young child.

21 Embellish a photo album with a cute baby design. Trim your stitched motif and stick it to contrasting card or fabric before attaching this to the cover of your album (see page 93). I covered my album with pretty matching fabric first (see page 95). Draw a child's name out on graph paper before you start stitching (see page 91).

Design size 10.75 x 5.75cm (4½ x 2¼in)
Stitch count 57 x 31

22 Stitch a child's name on Aida band (see page 91) and sew this to a small drawstring bag for holding a christening gift. You can either make your own bag (see page 96) or buy one from a high street shop instead. You can also decorate a child's towelling hooded robe in the same way.

Design size letter as shown
3.75 x 3.75cm (1½ x 1½in)
Stitch count 21 x 22

23 This colourful play cube adorned with tiny teddies and numbers is a soft and cuddly way to start baby off on the road to learning (see page 97 for making up instructions). Each teddy letter only takes a couple of hours to stitch, making them ideal for quick gift tags or cards as well.

Design size for each design,
approximately 2.5 x 4.75cm (1 x 1½in)
Stitch count 13 x 21

DMC stranded cotton
Cross stitch

Backstitch

208	729	818	3609	3851	— 780
210	745	964	3805	3855	
647	761	996	○ 3823		

DMC stranded cotton
Cross stitch

Backstitch

208	729	818	3609	3851
210	745	964	3805	3855
647	761	996	○ 3823	

— 780

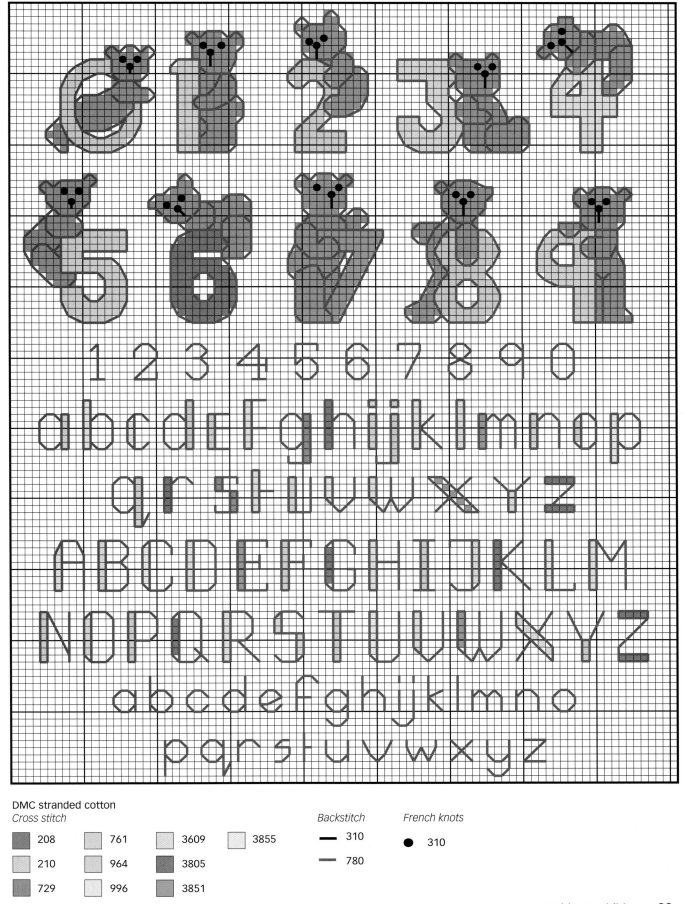

DMC stranded cotton

Cross stitch

208	761	3609	3855
210	964	3805	
729	996	3851	

Backstitch

— 310

— 780

French knots

● 310

Weddings & Anniversaries

A wedding is a day to remember, when the finishing touches and details make all the difference. In this chapter you will find lots of pretty, romantic gifts to make for everyone involved.

These include a special band for a wedding cake, a pretty brooch for the mother of the bride, and a sachet for a young bridesmaid to hold. Many of the motifs on each page can be made into a number of different gifts and keepsakes, or stitched as last-minute tags.

The milestone wedding anniversaries – silver, ruby and gold – are easy to remember, but can you name the other years in between? Surprise your friends and family with a personalized gift on their anniversary. There are lots of designs and gift ideas to choose from, including some to stitch for specific wedding anniversaries, such as a wooden treasure box, a crystal trinket pot and a special finishing touch for a delicate china plant pot.

Create quick-to-stitch gifts and keepsakes for the happy couple's wedding celebration. For those already married, an anniversary gift will be the perfect token of their time together.

For the big day

These wedding gifts are easy to make and can be adapted
to suit the bride's special colour scheme.

24

A pretty rose motif makes
the perfect finishing touch
for a wedding album. The
design was stitched on 2in
(5cm) cream linen band
with a scalloped edge and
sewn to the album as
explained on page 94. Use
the alphabet on page 39 to
stitch the couple's initials.
This design would also
make a delightful bookmark
(see page 94).

Design size 3.75 x 10.5cm (1½ x 4⅛in)
Stitch count 21 x 61

Design size 3 x 3.75cm
(1¼ x 1½in)
Stitch count 18 x 20

25

Young bridesmaids will love to carry a
heart-shaped sachet on the day. Choose
thread colours and ribbon to match their
outfit and cover the seam with beaded cord
for a special finishing touch. See page 98
for how to make a padded sachet.

26

Make a ring cushion using
this simple yet effective
wedding design. Choose a
linen or Aida background
fabric to match your colour
scheme and trim with a gold
beaded edging. Complete the
cushion in the same way as a
sachet (see page 98) and sew
on some matching narrow
ribbon to keep the rings safe.

Design size 7.5 x 7.5cm (3 x 3in)
Stitch count 41 x 41

DMC stranded cotton
Cross stitch

• blanc	322	I 746	813	3347	Kreinik gold HL 002		
164	676	760	3072	✓ 3822			
O 225	677	761	3328	3823			

Backstitch
— 433
— 904
— 3328
— DMC Art 273
— Kreinik gold HL 002

French knots
○ 813
● 3328
○ 3821

The finishing touches

These wedding motifs and repeating borders are ideal for making small gifts and tags, and for stitching on linen and Aida bands to decorate the wedding cake.

27 A hand stitched floral brooch will make the perfect gift for the mother of the bride (see page 102). I worked one of the tiny floral motifs on 28-count cream Brittney linen and put it in a gold oval brooch. These small motifs will also look good on a handbag mirror or in the lid of a trinket pot.

Design size 2 x 2.75cm (⅞ x 1⅛in)
Stitch count 10 x 17

Design size
shoe, 3.75 x 2.5cm (1½ x 1in); heart, 3.5 x 3.5cm (1⅜ x 1⅜in)
Stitch count
shoe, 19 x 14; heart, 18 x 20

28 Complete your bridesmaids' gifts with specially stitched tags. The motifs were stuck on to card and attached with matching ribbon to a gift bag and gift box (see page 94). Choose thread colours to match the wedding colour scheme.

Design size *for one motif* 5.75 x 3.5cm (2¼ x 1⅜in)
Stitch count *for one motif* 32 x 18

29 A rose band makes a simple yet stylish decoration for the wedding centrepiece – the cake. Many of the repeating border motifs on this page are designed for stitching on Aida or linen band in this way (see page 91). When attaching your band to the cake make sure the design is the right way up (see page 97).

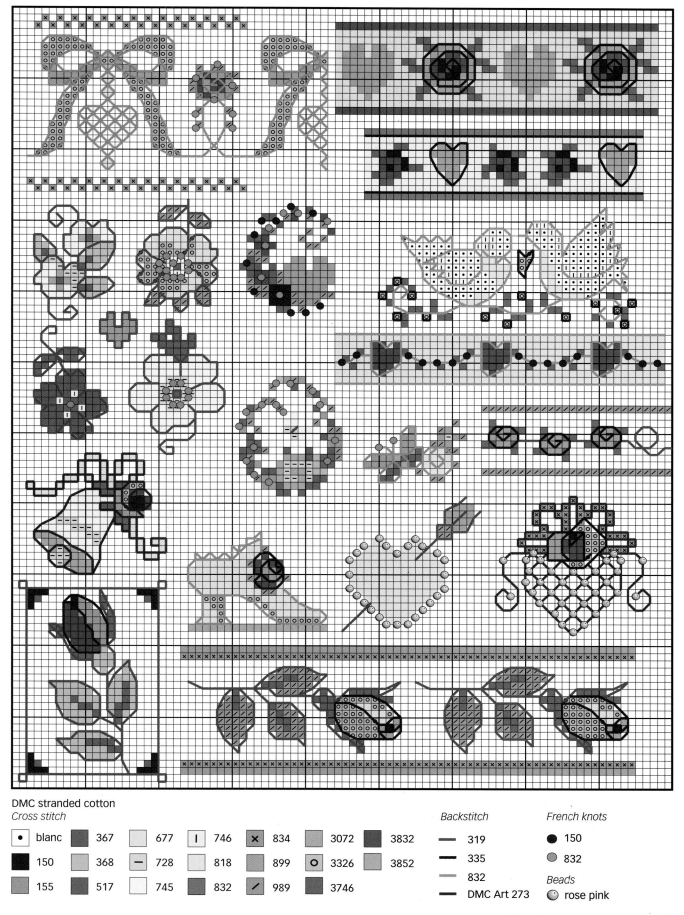

DMC stranded cotton

Cross stitch

• blanc	367	677	I 746	✕ 834	3072	3832
150	368	− 728	818	899	3326	3852
155	517	745	832	╱ 989	3746	

Backstitch

— 319
— 335
— 832
— DMC Art 273

French knots

● 150
● 832

Beads
◐ rose pink

Anniversary gifts

Here you will find small and larger designs to stitch for an anniversary.

30 **This pretty photo frame** will make a charming first anniversary gift. The design was stitched on pale blue Aida and then used to cover a card mount with an aperture cut out of the centre (see page 101). Beads add the finishing touches.

Design size 16 x 20.5cm (6⅜ x 8in)
Stitch count 88 x 107

31 An elegant trinket pot will make a special silver wedding gift – and only needs a simple motif to set it off a treat. This pretty design is quick to stitch and can be worked in silver metallic thread instead of Anchor Reflecta if you prefer (see page 102 for suppliers).

Design size
2.5 x 3cm (1 x 1¼in)
Stitch count 12 x 15

32 **Make a special tag** to go with a ruby or golden wedding anniversary gift. The designs were stitched on Aida, which was trimmed to size and fringed before being stuck to a piece of card with a hole punched in the corner for a string or ribbon. These designs are perfect for other occasions too.

Design size *red rose* 2 x 8.2cm (⅞ x 3¼in);
yellow rose 5 x 5cm (2 x 2in)
Stitch count *red rose* 11 x 44; *yellow rose* 27 x 27

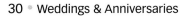

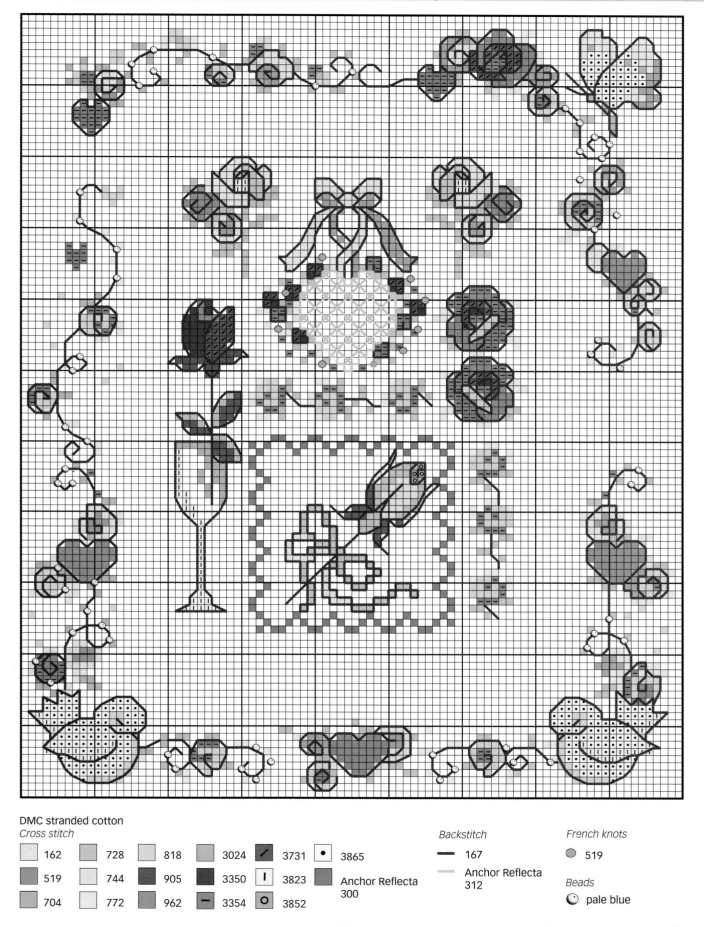

DMC stranded cotton
Cross stitch

162	728	818	3024	╱ 3731	● 3865
519	744	905	3350	Ι 3823	Anchor Reflecta 300
704	772	962	3354	O 3852	

Backstitch
— 167
Anchor Reflecta 312

French knots
○ 519

Beads
�◐ pale blue

For a special day

An anniversary is a special occasion that calls for one of these perfect momentos.

33 A glass paperweight containing a stitched dove carrying a scroll of paper will make a charming first anniversary gift. The design was stitched on 28-count pale blue Cashel linen and mounted face up in the paperweight base (see page 102). You could also make it into a card or tag (see page 93) and attach it to pretty stationery instead.

Design size 4.5 x 3cm (1¾ x 1¼in)
Stitch count 23 x 17

34 This delightful pair of swans makes a romantic design for the lid of a wooden box (see page 102). The motif is worked on 14-count Aida using only a handful of colours and will make a relaxing weekend project for every stitcher. Cut your finished design larger than the box aperture and slide it into place.

Design size
7.3 x 4cm (2⅞ x1⅝in)
Stitch count 39 x 22

You can stitch the swans and floral wreath motifs for any anniversary. Simply add the correct number of years using the alphabet on page 39.

1	Paper	**9**	Copper	**20**	China
2	Cotton	**10**	Tin	**25**	Silver
3	Leather	**11**	Steel	**30**	Pearl
4	Books	**12**	Silk	**35**	Coral
5	Wood	**13**	Lace	**40**	Ruby
6	Iron	**14**	Ivory	**45**	Sapphire
7	Wool	**15**	Crystal	**50**	Golden
8	Bronze				

Design size
5.2 x 5.2cm (2 x 2in)
Stitch count
29 x 29

35 A crystal bowl makes an ideal gift for a fifteenth anniversary (see page 102) – especially when this simple design is stitched in beautiful Reflecta metallic threads on 28-count pale blue Cashel linen. Use one strand for the cross stitch and one strand for the backstitch.

DMC stranded cotton
Cross stitch

• blanc	— 169	⬛ 310	703	761	╲ 3756	3833	⊙ Anchor Reflecta 312	
162	— 225	517	743	827	3826	3853	╱ Anchor Reflecta 316	
168	300	702	744	3078	3832			

Backstitch
— 300
— Anchor Reflecta 316

French knots
● 310

Precious memories

Here are some more gorgeous gifts to make for an anniversary.

Design size 4.5 x 4.5cm
(1¾ x 1¾ in)
Stitch count 25 x 25

Design size 9.5 x 4cm (3¾ x 1⅝in)
Stitch count 52 x 21

36

This swan plant poke will make a charming gift for a china anniversary. It was stitched on butter cream perforated paper, but you can also use plastic canvas (see page 91). The trimmed motif was stuck to a lolly stick with double-sided tape.

37

A basket decorated with a stitched band (see page 91) and filled with bathroom goodies will make a thoughtful anniversary gift. I have stitched the design for a sixth anniversary, but it is suitable for any other year as well. You can also make it into a tag using perforated paper instead of fabric (see page 93).

DMC stranded cotton

Cross stitch

◉ 310	422	704	905	3756	3833		
333	╱ 535	725	963	3799	− 3865		
340	647	╲ 729	3072	3823			
✕ 347	676	• 746	◯ 3326	3832			

Backstitch
— 333
— 347
— 898
— 3865

French knots
● 310
● 347
● 704

Love letters

Use the letters from this scrolled alphabet to make stylish quick gifts for a wedding couple.

38 **Make matching initialled bags** for holding confetti at a wedding. I stitched the letters B and G for bride and groom, but you can choose from the alphabet opposite. I used 28-count platinum Cashel linen fabric and trimmed my bags with broderie anglaise. See page 96 for how to make up the bags.

Design size and **stitch count** will vary with each letter

Design size
5 x 14cm (2 x 5½in)
Stitch count 28 x 79

39 A wedding bell pull stitched with a couple's initials and the date of their wedding is sure to become a treasured keepsake. Draw the letters and motifs out on graph paper before you start stitching. I used the same fabric and lace edging as for the gift above. See page 96 for how to make up a bellpull.

Design size and **Stitch count** will vary with each letter

40 **When you need a** special gift but have little time left for stitching, a gold bell frame filled with a delicate stitched initial will fit the bill (see page 102). I used the same linen fabric as before but you can match the bride's colour scheme instead.

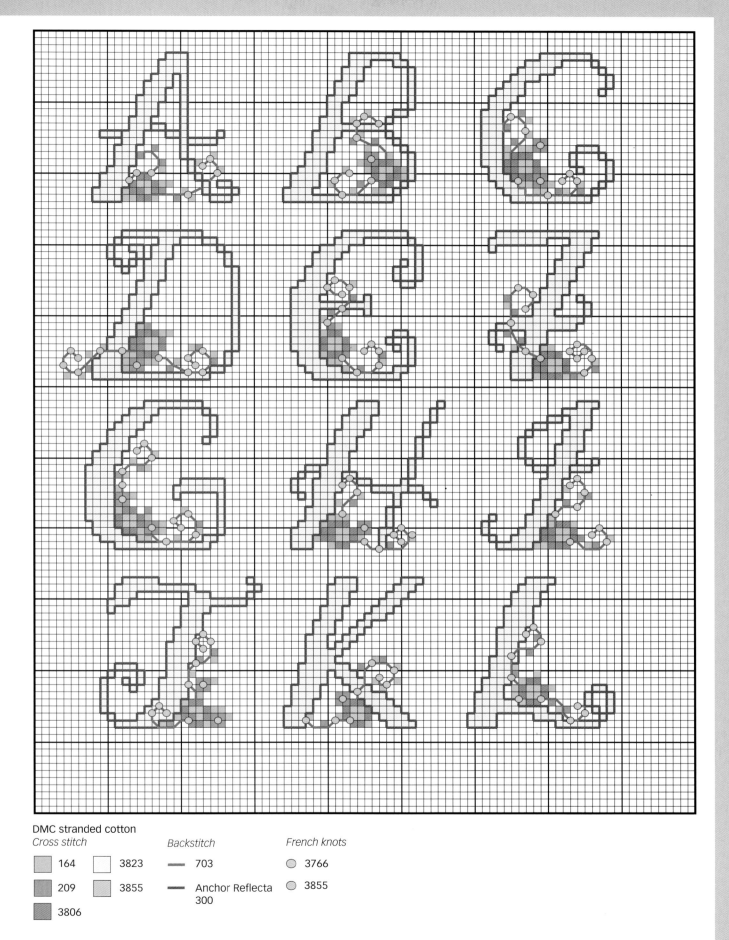

DMC stranded cotton

Cross stitch

	164		3823
	209		3855
	3806		

Backstitch

— 703

— Anchor Reflecta 300

French knots

○ 3766

○ 3855

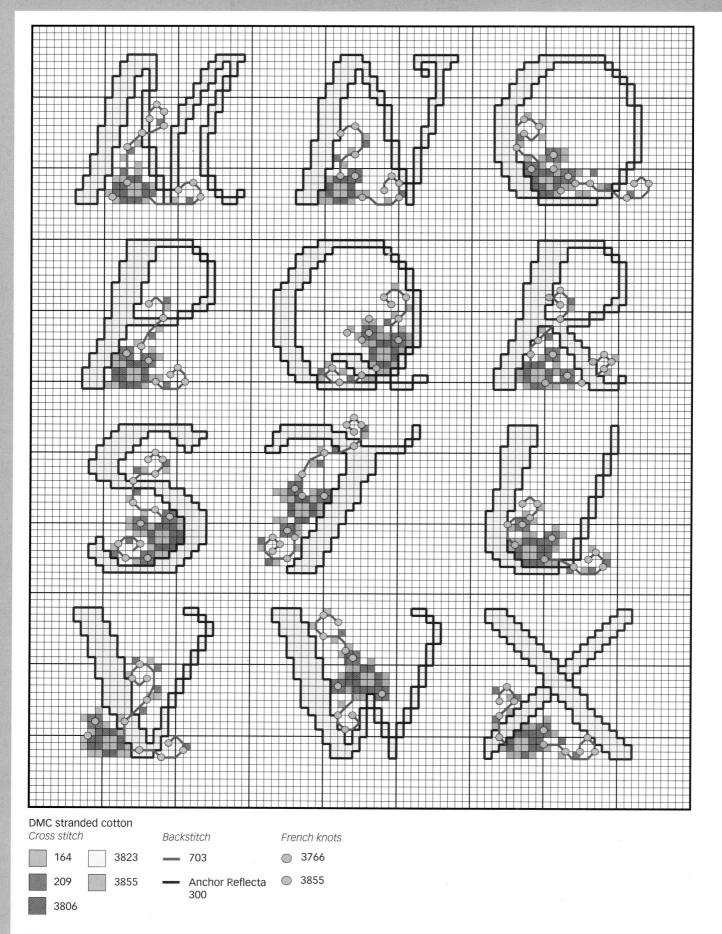

DMC stranded cotton

Cross stitch

▢ 164	▢ 3823	
▢ 209	▢ 3855	
▨ 3806		

Backstitch

— 703

— Anchor Reflecta 300

French knots

◯ 3766

◯ 3855

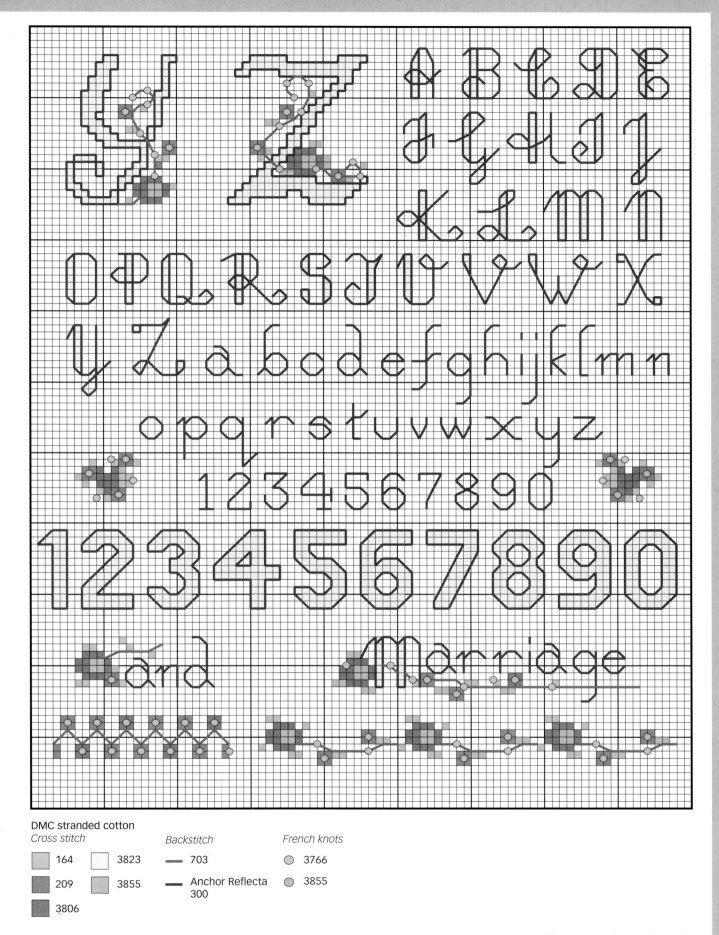

DMC stranded cotton

Cross stitch

▨ 164	▢ 3823		
▨ 209	▨ 3855		
▨ 3806			

Backstitch

— 703

▬ Anchor Reflecta 300

French knots

○ 3766

● 3855

Days to Remember

Celebrate a special day with a hand stitched gift. In this chapter you will find plenty of designs to wish friends and family well in a new venture and for lots of other occasions.

Three country cottage motifs are ideal for filling the sides of a noteblock as a new-home gift. A good luck keyring attached to a cute teddy makes a charming farewell gift for a friend who's leaving for pastures new. Do you know someone who's graduating soon? Make a starry frame to hold their graduation photo or a wise owl bookmark to congratulate them on their success.

An eighteenth birthday calls for a special gift. Add a lucky black cat motif to the cover of an album for holding photos of the birthday night out. You will find lots of other fun birthday motifs, and gifts to make with them, for both men and women of all ages. But why wait for their birthday to treat your family and friends to a unique handstitched gift?

Mark the occasion with a special gift, whether you are welcoming a friend to their new home or celebrating a milestone birthday.

New home welcome

Help friends and family settle into their new home by making these delightful and practical gifts for them.

Design size 15.5 x 3.5cm (6⅛ x 1⅜in)
Stitch count 85 x 19

41

A decorated hand towel will make a thoughtful housewarming present. The pretty motif was stitched in the centre of a cream Aida band (see page 91) and sewn to the edge of a towel (see page 97).

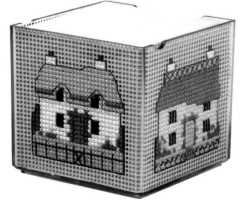

42

A plant poke makes an unusual gift idea and is quick to stitch. The folk style birdhouse was worked on plastic canvas, a handy material which doesn't fray and can be cut to shape afterwards (see page 91). The finished motif was stuck to a lolly stick with double-sided tape.

Design size
3.5 x 5.5cm (1⅜ x 2¼)
Stitch count 20 x 30

Design size *for each cottage*
approximately 4.5 x 4.5cm (1¾ x 1¾in)
Stitch count 25 x 25

43

Decorate a noteblock on three sides with cottages (see page 102). The designs can be stitched on either fabric or perforated paper (see page 92) before being trimmed to fit the apertures. Back your fabric with iron-on interfacing to stop it fraying after stitching. The designs will also make charming quick cards.

DMC stranded cotton

Cross stitch

151	435	680	/ 818	− 869	3756
310	676	704	826	− 905	3833
350	677	✕ 728	827	3348	• blanc

Backstitch

— 310
— 869
— blanc

French knots

● 310

Hip, hip, hooray!

Stitch one of these designs to wish someone good luck, bon voyage or to congratulate them on their exam success.

Design size and **Stitch count** will vary.

44 Make a special frame with a stitched mount to hold a graduation photo. I put the scroll in the bottom right corner and added further stars all round. My design was stitched on 14-count khaki Aida with DMC Art 273 gold metallic thread for the backstitch. Plan your design on graph paper first (see page 91). See page 101 for how to make up your frame.

45

Stitch a good luck bookmark for a student who is about to take their exams. I worked my design on perforated paper (see page 91) combining several motifs charted opposite and letters from the alphabet on page 39. Glue coloured paper to the reverse side to neaten it and for writing your message.

Design size *for owl motif only* 4.5 x 8.2cm
Stitch count 25 x 42

46 A luggage label or key ring makes an excellent gift for a traveller (see page 102). The design was stitched on perforated paper, backed with white paper and trimmed to fit the key ring aperture. Check your design is correctly positioned before you snap the key ring shut because you won't be able to open it again.

Design size
3.5 x 3cm (1⅜ x 1¼in)
Stitch count 20 x 17

DMC stranded cotton

Cross stitch

• blanc	436	743	798	919	3348	❙ 3852
310	470	747	✓ 824	3072	3799	✓ 3855
◎ 422	676	▬ 780	900	3346	3823	

Backstitch
— 310
— 801
— 3345

French knots
● 310

Celebrate the Year

There are many occasions when a small stitched gift will mean so much to the person who receives it. In this chapter you will find designs to make for Mother's Day, Easter, Thanksgiving, the Chinese New Year and other celebrations throughout the year.

The Mother's Day motifs on page 62 are stitched in soft, pretty shades of pink and blue, and make wonderful sachets and drawstring bags you can fill with pot pourri. Don't forget your dad on Father's Day, too. A fishy paperweight and a gardening sampler are among the fun gifts to make for dads. Easter is the perfect occasion to stitch pretty spring motifs as cards, tags or a cakeband for a Simnel cake.

There are gorgeous fruity gifts to celebrate the harvest and fun, spooky badges for Halloween. You can also stitch the Chinese astrological signs for New Year. Your family and friends will love your thoughtful gifts.

There are lots of celebrations throughout the year that call for a lovely handmade gift. You'll find inspiration for every occasion in this chapter.

Mother's delight

Soft colours and pretty feminine motifs are
a must for Mother's Day.

Design size
7.5 x 9.5cm (3 x 3⅞in)
Stitch count 41 x 53

64

A dainty bellpull makes a delightful gift for
Mother's Day. The mini sampler design was
stitched on a wide white linen band with eyelet
holes (see page 102) and mounted on bellpull
ends (see page 96). You could also stitch the
design for a birthday or other occasion.

Design size
3.7 x 3.7cm (1½ x 1½in)
Stitch count 21 x 21

65

A scented sachet makes
a charming Mother's Day
gift. The fan design was
stitched on lilac Aida band
(see page 91), folded in half
and made into a sachet as
explained on page 98.

66

Make a drawstring bag to
fill with pot pourri using the
butterfly and lily of the valley
repeating motif opposite. I
stitched the design on pale
blue 28-count Cashel linen
and made it into a bag as
explained on page 96. Use a
length of ribbon to secure
the top. Refresh the pot
pourri regularly to keep your
clothes smelling sweet.

Design size 10 x 4.4cm (4 x 13/4in)
Stitch count 56 x 24

DMC stranded cotton
Cross stitch

151	211	518
208	225	725
209	310	727

734	907	3806	3823
747	3761	3814	B5200
905	905	3765	3820

Backstitch

— 211
— 610
— 905
— 3837

French knots

● 310
○ 3820

Just for dads

This fun selection of designs should help you find the right gift for Father's Day. There are more ideas for men's gifts on page 49.

67

This bellpull will make a charming gift for a keen gardener. It was stitched on 14-count rustico Aida and mounted on bellpull ends as explained on page 96. It would also look good on the cover of a notebook or diary (see page 93).

Design size
5 x 4.5cm (2 x 1⅞in)
Stitch count
26 x 25

Design size
6.51 x 13.2cm (2⅝ x 5¼in)
Stitch count 37 x 73

68

Make a useful paperweight as a gift for Father's Day (see page 102). I stitched the fish motif on 28-count colonial blue Cashel linen and trimmed it to fit the aperture. The ship is also the right size for a paperweight.

69

A desk set will make a special gift for a football fan or simply a number one dad. The design was also stitched on 28-count colonial blue Cashel linen, trimmed to size and mounted in the round aperture of the pen holder (see page 102).

Design size
4.5 x 5.1cm (1¾ x 2in)
Stitch count 23 x 28

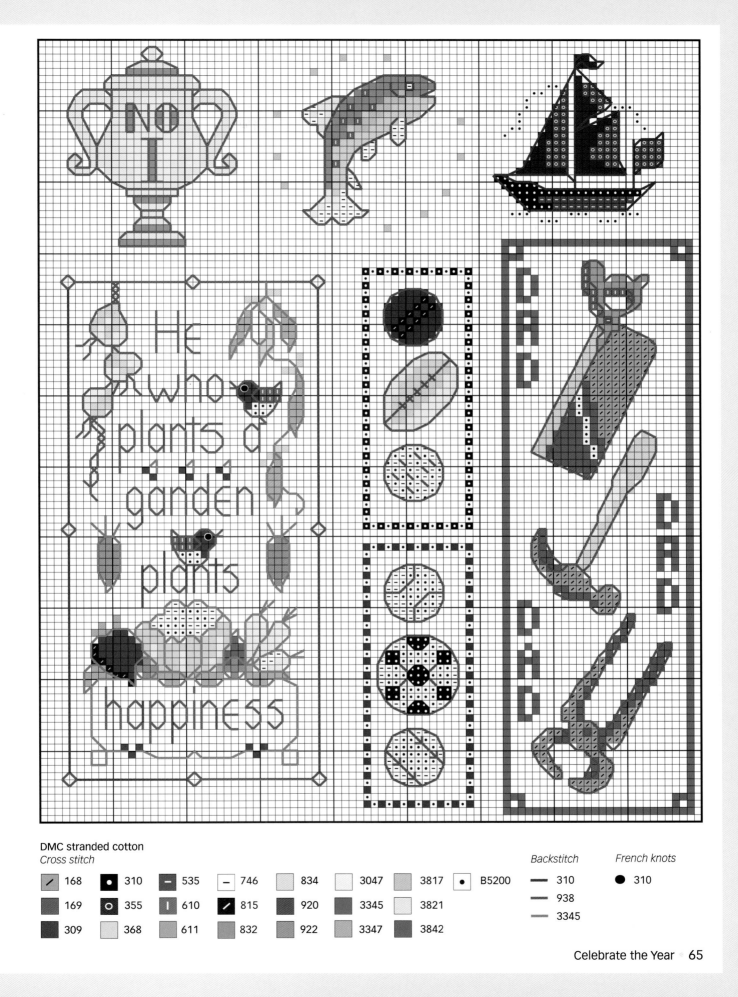

DMC stranded cotton
Cross stitch

✓ 168	■ 310	— 535	— 746	834	3047	3817	• B5200	
169	◉ 355	❙ 610	✓ 815	920	3345	3821		
309	368	611	832	922	3347	3842		

Backstitch
— 310
— 938
— 3345

French knots
● 310

Easter parade

Make a series of Easter gifts that will appeal to young and old alike using these pretty spring motifs.

Design size one repeat: 3.5 x 2cm (1¾ x ¾in)
Stitch count one repeat: 14 x 10

70

Cover an Easter cake with a band of pretty violets. I stitched the repeating violets motif on a strip of lemon linen fabric folded to size, but you can also use Aida band (see pages 91 and 94). The primrose or chick borders will also make attractive cakebands.

Design size
2.5 x 3.2cm (1 x 1¼in)
Stitch count 14 x 18

71

Make a child's Easter gift. I stitched the little rabbit motif on a 5cm (2in) wide strip of pale blue linen fabric, fringed the edges and tied it around bunny's neck as a cravatte.

Design size without border
4.2 x 4cm (1⅞ x 1¾in)
Stitch count without border 24 x 22

72

Decorate an Easter basket or another item you have bought. I added a primrose motif to the wooden heart tag attached to its handle. The design was stitched on cream perforated paper (see page 91), trimmed to shape and attached with double-sided tape (see page 93).

DMC stranded cotton
Cross stitch

▢ 151	▨ 333	▨ 422	▢ 742	▨ 907	▨ 3072	▨ 3607	▢ 3841
▨ 167	▨ 340	▢ 445	▬ 829	＼ 973	▬ 3078	▮ 3746	• B5200
▣ 310	▨ 350	▨ 718	▨ 906	▨ 976	▨ 3328	／ 3755	

Backstitch
— 310
— 333
— 829

French knots
● 310

Harvest festival

Stitch a series of designs evoking Autumn, the traditional time for abundance and thanksgiving.

73 Make a **fruity cover** and turn a jar of preserves into a special gift. I stitched my design on Aida and sewed this to a gingham circle (see page 100), but you can work the design directly on to the gingham using waste canvas as a grid if you prefer. The four fruit motifs can also be stitched on Aida band as an edging for a tray cloth or tea towel (see page 97).

Design size *for one motif* 3.5 x 3.5cm (1⅜ x 1⅜in)
Stitch count *for one motif* 19 x 19

74 Decorate a **cook's notebook** with a cornucopia design overflowing with fruit, flowers and vegetables. The motif was stitched on a square of Aida and fringed before being attached to the notebook with double-sided tape (see page 93).

Design size 7 x 7cm (2¾ x 2¾in)
Stitch count 38 x 38

75 Stitch a **folk art** design at Thanksgiving. These simple motifs look fresh and bright stitched on a red edged Aida band and sewn to a bright blue towel (see page 97).

Design size *for one motif* 7.5 x 4.5cm (3 x 1⅞in)
Stitch count 40 x 25

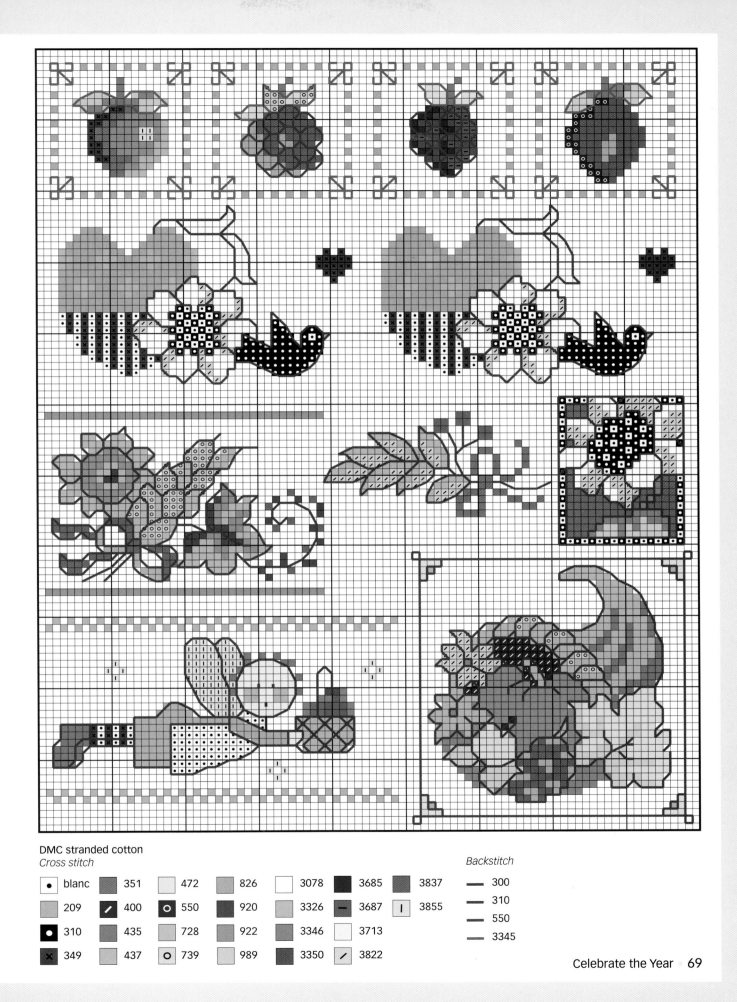

DMC stranded cotton
Cross stitch

Backstitch

• blanc	351	472	826	3078	3685	3837		— 300
209	/ 400	◉ 550	920	3326	— 3687	│ 3855		— 310
310	435	728	922	3346	3713			— 550
✕ 349	437	○ 739	989	3350	/ 3822			— 3345

Halloween fun

Send a spooky greeting using one of these Halloween designs or make them into fun badges and bags for trick-or-treating expeditions.

76 These simple Halloween motifs make wonderful cards or tags (see page 93–4). Use two strands of Reflecta thread for the cross stitch and one strand of Art 273 for the backstitch against a red or black background to add a little sparkle.

Design size and stitch count varies with each motif

Design size
ghost 3.2 x 5cm (1⅛ x 1¾in);
hat 4.5 x 4.75cm (1⅞ x 2in)
Stitch count
ghost 16 x 25; *hat* 26 x 26

77 Children will love wearing these fun badges on Halloween. I stitched my designs on plastic canvas (see page 91), backed them with iron-on interfacing, then cut carefully round them and attached a safety pin. The ghost will certainly shine at night if you use pearl metallic thread (Kreinik pearl 032). Use one strand for the cross stitch and one strand of Art 273 for the backstitch.

Design size *frog* 3.5 x 3.5cm, (1⅜ x 1⅜in); *pumpkin* 4 x 3.5cm (1⅝ x 1⅜in)
Stitch count *frog* 22 x 20; *pumpkin* 24 x 21

78 These Halloween pocket money bags are stitched on red and black Aida band in metallic Reflecta thread. Use two strands for the cross stitch and one strand for the backstitch. Choose a deep shade of fabric to make the metallic threads sparkle. Instructions on how to make a bag are on page 96.

DMC stranded cotton
Cross stitch

T ecru	— 350	535	741	◉ 869	3047	/ Anchor Reflecta 300	• Kreinik Very Fine #4 Braid pearl 032		
166	422	647	○ 742	○ 869	3024	\ Anchor Reflecta 313			
● 310	470	725	✕ 817	I 3045	3713	/ Anchor Reflecta 314			

Backstitch

— 935

— DMC Art 273 antique gold

— Anchor Reflecta 314

National days

Here's a fun selection of quick gifts to stitch for the Chinese New Year, St Patrick's Day and the Fourth of July.

79 A fridge magnet is a lovely way to display your handiwork and makes a fun, quick gift for a friend (see page 102). I stitched my designs on perforated paper (see page 91) and trimmed them to fit the fridge magnet.

Design size and **Stitch count** will vary with each motif.

Design size and **Stitch count** will vary with each motif.

80 Make a key ring for a friend using the Chinese astrological sign for the year of their birth (see table). I worked my designs on perforated paper but you can also use 14-count Aida. Trim the design to fit the aperture and check it is correctly positioned before snapping shut. All of the motifs charted here are the right size for a key ring (see page 102).

Rat	Ox	Tiger	Rabbit	Dragon	Snake
1948	1949	1950	1951	1952	1953
1960	1961	1962	1963	1964	1965
1972	1973	1974	1975	1976	1977
1984	1985	1986	1987	1988	1989
1996	1997	1998	1999	2000	2001
Horse	**Ram**	**Monkey**	**Rooster**	**Dog**	**Pig**
1954	1955	1956	1957	1958	1959
1966	1967	1968	1969	1970	1971
1978	1979	1980	1981	1982	1983
1990	1991	1992	1993	1994	1995
2002	2003	2004	2005	2006	2007

You can find out more about Chinese astrology from your local library or by searching on the internet.

Design size 5.5 x 4.5cm (2¼ x 1¾in) **Stitch count** 30 x 24

81 Small frames are perfect for displaying the Chinese astrological signs. Two styles are pictured – a small square brass frame and a pendant frame (see page 102). The designs were stitched on 28-count cream Cashel linen and mounted following the manufacturer's instructions.

RAT

OX

TIGER

RABBIT

DRAGON

SNAKE

HORSE

RAM

MONKEY

ROOSTER

DOG

PIG

ST PATRICKS

OLD GLORY

NEW YEAR

DMC stranded cotton
Cross stitch

● 310	I 352	642	— 680	729	■ 869	
312	353	648	702	O 743	／ 3774	
349	369	677	703	746	● B5200	

Backstitch
— 310
— 349
— 702
— 898

Gifts for Christmas

At this time of year we think of peace, love, family and friends, as well as giving. In this chapter you will find lots of quick festive motifs and inspiring gift ideas to combine for memorable festive presents. Each page of charts has a different theme to help you choose easily.

We all have favourite decorations we like to bring out at Christmas. The robin and wreath cardholder on page 76 is easy to make and is sure to be treasured in this way. You will also find different ways to make hangings for your tree, including stockings, padded sachets and festive gold frames.

A hand stitched tag can transform a simple gift, such as a set of candles, into something special. You will find lots of motifs, both cute and traditional, to stitch as tags, and stylish ways to use them, like the Santa gift box on page 78.

Christmas is a time for making personalized presents that mean so much, like the little Advent gift bags on page 87. These quick motifs will make it so easy to stitch your own festive gifts and tags.

Last-minute Christmas shopping will be a thing of the past with these festive goodies. With so many gift ideas, you will always have something special to put under the tree, no matter how late you leave it!

74

Festive favourites

Use these traditional festive motifs to make a handy card holder and some beautiful gifts for the table.

Design size *for one repeat*
11.5 x 3.75cm (4½ x 1½in)
Stitch count 64 x 18

A cake decorated with a beautiful stitched band makes the perfect gift for a teatime visit at Christmas. Use three strands for the cross stitch on Aida band (see page 91) and finish off your cakeband as explained on page 97.

82

83

These elegant festive napkins and napkin rings are stitched with a simple snowflake motif (see page 98). I used green 28-count Annabelle fabric, but another dark colour will look just as effective. You can stitch each guest's initial from the alphabet on page 89 instead of a snowflake if you prefer.

For each napkin
Design size *for a single snowflake*
3.75 x 3.75cm (1½ x 1½in)
Stitch count 17 x 17

For each napkin ring
Design size 10.75 x 3.75cm (4¼ x 1½in)
Stitch count 61 x 17

Design size
5.75 x 5.75cm (2¼ x 2¼in)
Stitch count 31 x 31

84

This garland card hanger will make a practical way to display your cards tidily. The design was stitched on 14-count Aida and made up as explained on page 99. Why not stitch the design again to use on your Christmas cards as well?

DMC stranded cotton

Cross stitch

• blanc	349	703	744	3852	
310	350	728	3756		
347	701	○ 742	3826		

Backstitch

— 310
— 699
— 801

French knots

● 349
● 3852

Season's greetings

Make your own festive tags and labels from perforated paper using these fun quick motifs.

85

These cheeky characters add a fun finishing touch to small crackers. I stitched the designs on green perforated paper (see page 91) and trimmed close to the edge of each one before sticking it to a cracker with double-sided tape. There are other shades of stitching paper to choose from.

Design size
3.25 x 3.75cm (1¼ x 1½in)
Stitch count 17 x 21

Design size
and **Stitch
count** varies
with each motif

86

Stitch an appropriate tag for a Christmas pudding as a special gift for Christmas Day. The design was worked on red perforated paper and stuck to a square of yellow card punched with a hole in one corner for the ribbon (see page 93).

Design size and
Stitch count varies
with each motif

87

Hand stitched tags will make your festive gifts a pleasure to open. This Santa was worked on perforated paper and stuck to matching card (see page 93). You can also decorate smaller gift boxes in the same way with your own stitched tag to hang on the tree.

DMC stranded cotton
Cross stitch

• blanc	⁄ 350	701	742	780	3756
310	517	703	ı 743	948	3799
349	676	725	761	976	

Backstitch

— 310

— Art 273 antique gold

French knots

● 310

● 349

Truly traditional

Sparkling Christmas tree motifs are used to make pretty tags and decorations.

88 Shining gold frames in the shape of a tree, a star and a bell (see page 102) are perfect for displaying Christmas designs. They can either be hung on the tree or used as special tags for larger gifts. The designs were stitched on red perforated paper and are easy to assemble in the frames following the manufacturer's instructions. For more sparkle use gold perforated paper.

Design size and **Stitch count** varies with each motif.

Design size and **Stitch count** varies with each motif.

Design size and **Stitch count** varies with each motif.

89 These simple sachets, filled with lavender or pot pourri, and decorated with a stitched tag (see page 93) will make a charming festive gift for a friend. I made my sachets from pretty gold fabric (see page 98), tied them with matching ribbon and stitched the holly leaves in gold metallic thread on red perforated paper (see page 91).

90 Trim a candle with a festive motif to make a special gift. I stitched the poinsettia design on 9cm (2½in) Aida band and wrapped this around a large matching candle (see page 97). Or you can stitch a tag to hang from a bundle of festive candles tied with ribbon. I trimmed and fringed my fabric then stuck it to a folded piece of coloured card (see page 93) .

DMC stranded cotton

Cross stitch

• blanc	701	I 922	3847	
347	/ 728	3801	3852	
400	917	3837	5282 metallic	

Backstitch

— Art 273 antique gold

Away in a manger

These lovely gifts stitched with traditional motifs are in keeping with the simple message of the Nativity.

91 These padded animal hearts edged with checked fabric will look gorgeous hanging on a Christmas tree or over a baby's cot. Instructions on how to make them are on page 98.

Design size approximately 2.5 x 2.5cm (1 x 1in)
Stitch count *donkey* 15 x 15; *sheep* 14 x 13; *cow* 19 x 13; *horse* 16 x 14

92

Festive motifs stitched on cream linen band make the perfect decoration for papier mâché gift boxes in a natural shade (see page 97). I used a 4.5cm (1¾in) 28-count linen band (see page 91) and added matching ribbon around the lid.

Design size *angel* 5.75 x 3.75cm (2¼ x 1½in); *shepherds* 6.4 x 4.5cm (2½ x 1¾in)
Stitch count *angel* 30 x 21; *shepherds* 34 x 25

93

Design size 7 x 7cm (2¾ x 2¾in)
Stitch count 39 x 39

The little animal sampler can be used to make lots of different gifts. I made it into a cover for a small notebook by attaching my trimmed and fringed stitched design to the front (see page 93). A matching bookmark was made with just the sheep motif which was framed with a card mount and attached to ribbon.

Design size 9 x 4.5cm (3½ x 1¾in)
Stitch count 47 x 25

94

The Three Wise Men motif makes an attractive design for a guest towel for Christmas visitors. This stylized trio is stitched in beautiful shades of gold, mauve and turquoise on 28-count linen band and sewn to a contrasting coloured towel (see page 97).

DMC stranded cotton
Cross stitch

▨ 208	▬ 422	⊙ 744	928
225	676	■ 898	3022
▣ 310	738	917	3024

3325	✱ 3821	5282 metallic
3814	3828	
3820	• 3865	

Backstitch

▬▬ 898

▬▬ Art 273 antique gold

Around the tree

Who can resist making some of these cute quick festive tags, sachets and stockings?

95 These small sachets decorated with stitched motifs and ribbon ties will make wonderful thank-you gifts or tree hangings. They are made from Christmas fabric and the fringed designs were glued in place (see page 98). If you fill them with a pot pourri or spice mixture they can be used to scent a drawer afterwards.

Design size
squirrel, cat, rabbit
2.5 x 3.2cm (1 x 1¼in);
robin 3.2 x 3.2cm
(1¼ x 1¼in);
Stitch count *squirrel, cat, rabbit* 14 x 17;
robin 16 x 15

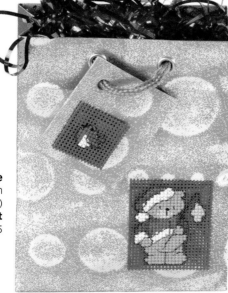

96 Personalize a gift sack with your own stitched tag. I stitched the cute teddies on green perforated paper (see page 91) and stuck them on with double-sided tape. My bag came with its own gift tag to which I added the little robin.

Design size
3.75 x 4.5cm
(1½ x 1¾in)
Stitch count
20 x 25

97 Cute little stockings are ideal for filling with sweets and hanging from the tree, or for containing a small present for a child. Making up instructions are on page 101. I stitched my angels on red Aida using gold metallic thread, but you can also stitch them for a birthday using pale fabric and yellow cotton.

Design size *standing angel*
3.75 x 5.75cm (1½ x 2¼in);
kneeling angel 2.5 x 5cm (1 x 2in)
Stitch Count *standing angel*
19 x 39; *kneeling angel* 15 x 27

DMC stranded cotton
Cross stitch

• blanc	434	I 712	761	911
◉ 310	/ 676	728	819	3801
349	700	729	906	5282 metallic

Backstitch

— 310
— 898
5282 metallic
— Art 273 antique gold

French knot

● 310
● 349

A Christmas message

Use the festive alphabet and advent calendar to make personalized coasters, gift bags and boxes.

98

This pretty wall hanging will send a special message of peace and love at Christmas. It is stitched in shades of Christmas red cotton on a 28-count linen band and suspended by a decorative bell pull (see page 96). You can also work this design on 14-count Aida fabric instead.

Design size
3.2 x 13.3cm
(1¼ x 5¼in)
Stitch count
18 x 72

99

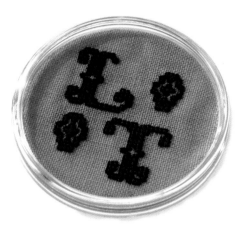

Stitch a coaster as an unusual Christmas gift to take to a dinner party. A couple of letters from the traditional alphabet have been arranged to fit inside a circular coaster (see page 102). Plan the arrangement of your letters on graph paper first (see page 91).

Design size 4.5 x 5.2cm (1¾ x 2¼in)
Stitch count 25 x 32

100

Use these little bags decorated with motifs from the advent calendar on page 88 to hide a set of individual Advent surprises. The bags are easy to make using Christmas fabric (see page 96) and the fringed motifs were simply glued to the front.

Design size and **Stitch count** varies with each motif

Design size and **Stitch count** varies with each motif

101

Stitch a design for the lid of a tiny trinket box that can be filled with sweets or hung from the tree. You can buy the boxes (see page 102) and either leave them plain or paint them in a pretty colour. You can also use the letters to add a child's name across the top of a festive stocking.

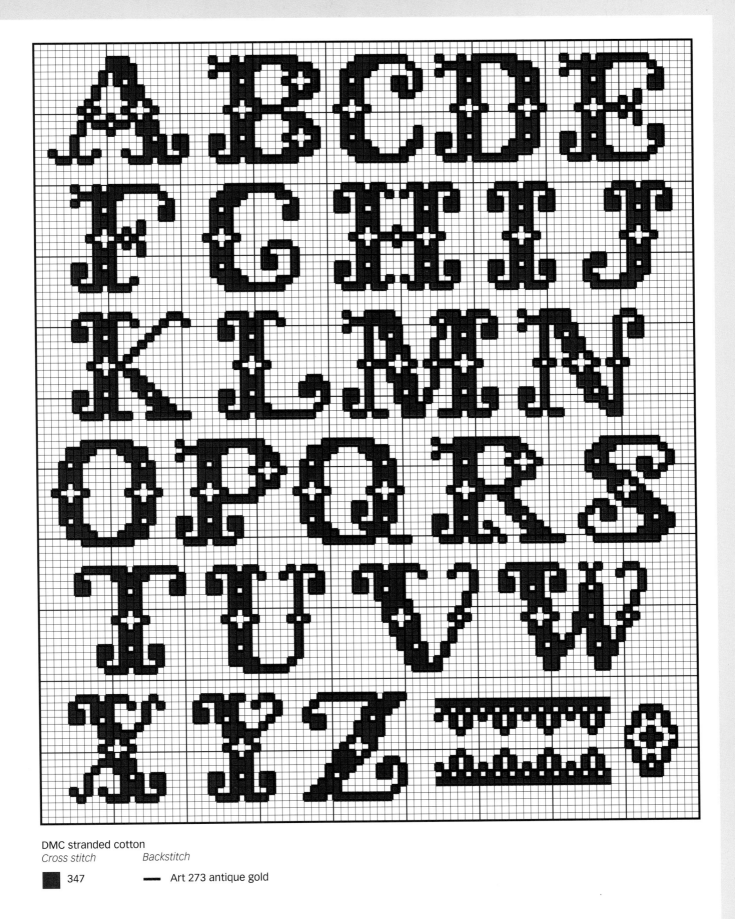

DMC stranded cotton

Cross stitch *Backstitch*

347 —— Art 273 antique gold

DMC stranded cotton
Cross stitch

• blanc	▬ 347	701	728	819	3024
⊙ 300	350	703	❘ 782	828	
301	402	725	813	╱ 922	

Backstitch
—— 300
(2 strands for letters and numbers, 1 strand elsewhere)

French knot
● 310
● 347

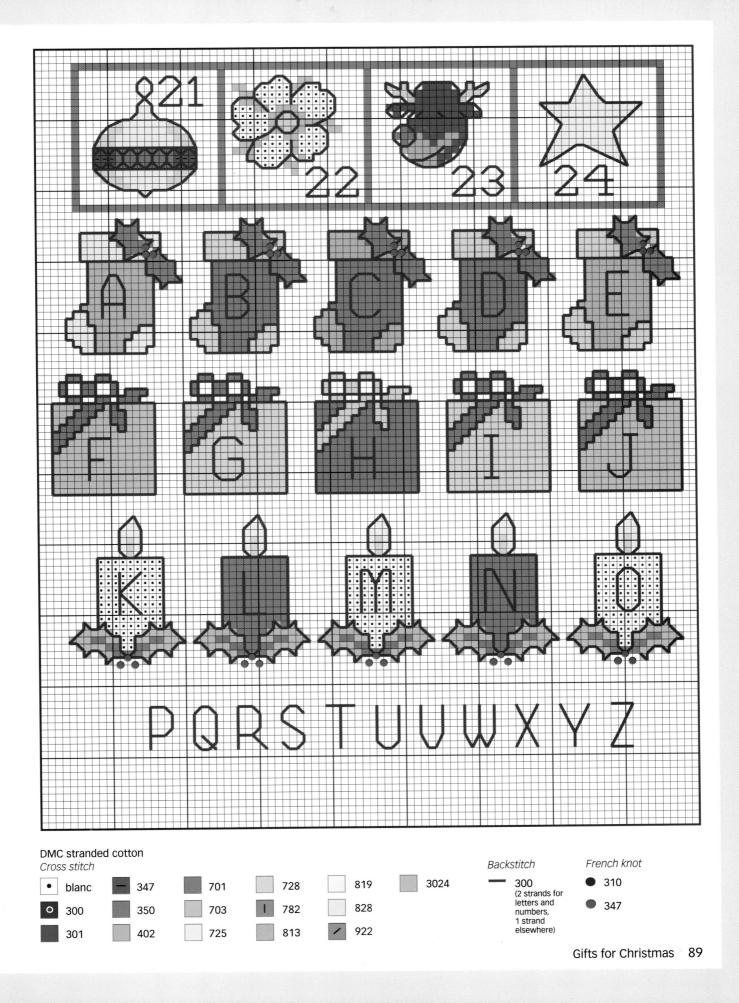

DMC stranded cotton

Cross stitch

• blanc	— 347	701	728
◉ 300	350	703		782
301	402	725	813

819	3024
828	
⁄ 922	

Backstitch

— 300
(2 strands for letters and numbers, 1 strand elsewhere)

French knot

● 310

● 347

Stitching Techniques

Here you will find all the information you need on stitching the designs in the book and the materials and equipment they require.

Fabric

Most of the designs in this book are stitched on Aida and evenweave fabrics. These have an equal number of horizontal and vertical threads in their weave, which makes them ideal for counted cross stitch designs worked from a chart.

On Aida, which is woven from blocks of threads, each cross stitch is worked over one block of threads using the holes as a guide. On linen, and other finer count evenweave fabrics, each cross stitch is worked over two threads of the fabric. Thus a project sewn over two threads on 28-count linen will come out the same size as it would stitched on 14-count Aida.

Where possible, I have given the design size and stitch count for the fabric used for each project. If you want to work the designs on other size fabrics you will need to calculate the finished size of the project. To do this, count the number of squares in both the height and width of your chosen design – this is the stitch count. Then divide the two measurements by the count, or number of threads per inch, of your fabric. This will give you the size in inches. When you are stitching over two threads remember to divide the stitch count by half the number of threads per inch.

Reading the charts

All the designs in the book are stitched from colour charts. Each coloured square on the chart represents a cross stitch worked over one block on Aida or over two threads on an evenweave fabric like linen. Some of the charts include three-quarter as well as whole cross stitches (these are also known as fractional stitches). These appear on the chart as coloured triangles.

Each chart has a key listing the threads used in numerical order. The key also shows if there is any backstitch outlining in the design, and if French knots or beads have been used. Backstitch and long stitch are shown on the charts by coloured outlines. Circles are used to indicate both French knots and beads, and these are clearly labelled.

Use two strands of stranded cotton (floss) for the cross stitch and three-quarter stitches and one strand for the backstitch on Aida or evenweave fabrics,

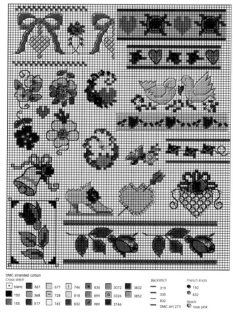

but see also Other Stitching Materials, opposite. Instructions for metallic threads appear alongside the projects.

Other stitching materials
Aida bands
I have stitched some of the projects using Aida and linen bands. These come with a pre-finished decorative edging which makes them easy to trim towels, bags and other items. These fabrics generally have a looser weave than ordinary Aida so you will need to stitch with more strands to produce nice plump stitches.

I recommend using three strands for the cross stitch, but work a practice sample in both two and three strands on a spare piece first to see which effect you prefer. Use two strands on linen bands. Spraying the back of Aida bands with spray starch will help to keep them firm for stitching.

Paper and plastic canvas
The same rules apply to perforated paper and plastic canvas, the other types of stitching material I have used. These rigid materials are ideal for making badges or tags for notebooks and cards, and are easy to stitch on, although plastic canvas is more durable. Choose a design that uses whole stitches only and has a simple shape that will be easy to cut round when completed.

Cut your plastic canvas or paper 5cm (2in) larger all the way round than the design. Measure the width and height and mark the centre with a pencil dot. Start stitching the design from the centre and work outward. Use three strands of cotton (floss) for the cross stitch and one strand for the backstitch.

When the stitching is complete trim the excess canvas or paper, either leaving a blank border or cutting carefully around the edge of the design. Use a small pair of general purpose craft scissors and leave one blank square all round to keep your stitches in place. You can back your design with coloured paper attached with double-sided tape.

Other equipment
Use a blunt tapestry needle for cross stitch in the correct size for your fabric count. This should slip easily through the holes in the fabric without enlarging or distorting them. A size 26 tapestry needle was used for the designs in this book and it should be fine enough to pass through the eye of most beads. If necessary a beading needle can be used instead.

Most of the designs are small enough to be stitched in your hand without using a frame or hoop. Remember to cut a large enough piece of fabric if you want to use one and trim the excess once the stitching is completed. Your project should always be removed from the frame when you have finished stitching to avoid a ring mark forming on the fabric.

Personalizing names and dates
Some cross stitch designs feature names and dates or other wording that you will need to alter using the alphabets provided. Before you begin to stitch, ensure the words will fit the space by counting the squares in the space available (both the width and height) and marking this on graph paper. Pencil the shape of the letters or numbers on the graph paper, spacing the letters and words correctly.

Washing and pressing
If you need to wash your work before mounting or making up, swish the stitching in lukewarm water with a little detergent. If any of the colours bleed, continue to rinse in fresh water until the water becomes clear. Roll the stitching in a clean towel and squeeze gently to remove most of the water. On a second towel, place your design face down, cover with a cloth and iron until dry. To prevent your stitching getting dirty always work with clean hands and keep drinks and food away from it.

Preparing to stitch
Organize the threads for a project before you start stitching. Cut your fabric several inches larger than the finished design size and oversew the edges to prevent fraying. Fold the fabric in half each way to find the centre point and mark this with a pin or a small stitch. Find the centre of your chosen motif on the chart and begin stitching from here.

Pull out the strands separately from a length of cotton (floss) then put together the number you need to thread your needle. Knot the end of the thread and push the needle to the back of the fabric about 3cm (1¼in) from your starting point. Leave the knot on the front of the fabric and stitch towards it. When you have covered enough of the thread on the back to secure it, cut off the knot and trim the end.

When you need to start a new colour, push the needle through the back of your stitches to secure the thread.

Working the stitches
Cross stitch
This is the main stitch used to create the designs. This is worked in two stages:

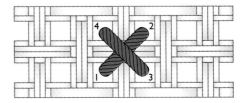

Fig 1a

first a diagonal stitch is worked over one block on Aida, then a second diagonal stitch is worked in the opposite direction on top forming a cross (Fig 1a), or over two threads on evenweave (Fig 1b). For a neat finish, make the top half of every cross stitch face the same direction.

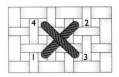

Fig 1b

If you have a large area to stitch in the same colour, you may prefer to work in rows instead of completing each cross stitch individually. Stitch a line of diagonal stitches, then turn round and work back again adding the top diagonal to each stitch (Fig 1c). This method produces neat lines of vertical stitching on the back that are useful for finishing off the thread ends.

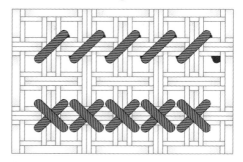

Fig 1c

Plan your route carefully around the chart, counting over short distances to avoid mistakes.

Three quarter cross stitch

These stitches add definition to a design and are useful for creating smoother curves or circles. They are shown on the charts by coloured triangles. Work a half cross stitch, then add a quarter stitch in the opposite direction, bringing the needle down in the centre of the half cross stitch you have just worked (Fig 2).

Fig 2

French Knots

These are used to add texture and detail to a design such as eyes or flower centres. They are worked in one or two strands of thread and are shown on the charts by a small coloured circle. Bring the needle up in the right place for the knot. Hold it down with your left thumb (if right handed) and wind the thread around the needle twice (see Fig 3a). Holding the thread taut, push the needle through to the back of the fabric, one thread or part of a block away from the entry point (see Fig 3b), forming a knot on the front. If you want a larger knot use more strands in the needle rather than wrapping the thread more times around the needle.

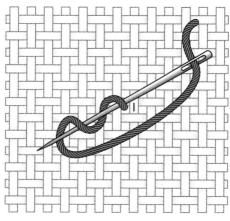

Fig 3a

Fig 3b

Backstitch

This stitch is the most effective way to add fine outlines for lettering designs. Bring the needle up, take it back one stitch length and then bring it up one stitch length beyond your starting point as shown (Fig 4). Always add these outlines after all the cross stitch has been completed to ensure they form solid lines.

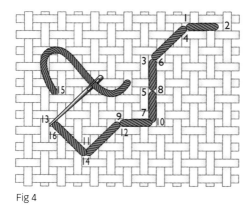

Fig 4

Beads

Bead positions are shown on the charts as coloured circles. Attach each bead with a half cross stitch using thread to match the bead colour (Fig 5). You can substitute seed beads for French knots if you prefer. Look for the closest match to the stranded cotton colours.

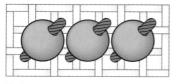

Fig 5

Making Up the Projects

Many of the gifts in this book have been mounted in products that are specially designed to display needlecraft. These include trinket pots, paperweights, a compact mirror, noteblock and a baby's sipper cup, as well as fridge magnets, key rings and coasters. Follow the manufacturer's easy instructions for making up these items. I have also used some of the ready-to-stitch wear, such as bibs. These come with an Aida panel for stitching a design on and again should be used following the manufacturer's instructions.

In this chapter you will find instructions on how to make up the other projects in the book. The techniques covered include making your stitched design into a tag, a drawstring bag, a cakeband, a sachet, a bellpull and a festive card holder. The steps are easy to follow and will help you to make your own stunning quick gifts your family and friends will love.

Stitched tags

A simple stitched tag can be attached with ribbon to make a gift look extra special, or used to decorate any number of different items such as an album, a gift box, a notebook or a child's cap (see pages 8, 16 and 18).

You will need
- Stitched motif
- Coloured card cut to size
- Double-sided tape

1 Trim your stitched fabric to fit your tag and fringe the edges. If using Aida band trim the length only.

2 Stick the fabric to the card with double-sided tape and punch a hole in one corner for a ribbon or string. You can also stick a design to the label on a gift box or basket you have bought – see the Easter basket on page 66.

3 You can stitch the design on perforated paper instead of fabric (see page 92). Or cut your fabric with pinking shears to give a decorated edge (see the baby album on page 95) and mount on contrasting coloured fabric instead of card.

4 To embellish the gift itself, stick your completed tag on an album, box or notebook using double-sided sticky tape.

Greeting cards

Many of the motifs in the book can be made into cards. You can either buy a pre-cut card mount with an aperture to fit your design or cut your own cards to match from a sheet of artist's card. You can personalize cards with beads, buttons and ribbons.

You will need
- Stitched design
- Card mount to fit
- Double-sided tape or craft glue

1 Trim the edges of your stitched fabric to fit inside the card aperture, leaving enough extra fabric for sticking in place.

2 Make sure the card is the right way up then apply a thin coat of craft glue or double-sided tape around the aperture on the back of the card (I prefer tape).

3 Lay the stitching face up on a flat surface and put the card on top. Check that the stitching is correctly positioned before pressing down firmly.

4 Fold the spare card flap over the back of the stitching and stick in place with glue or tape.

Embellished book covers

Work the motif on a strip of fabric and sew it around a book cover (see the recipe book on page 51 and the wedding album on page 27).

You will need
- Stitched motif
- Album or notebook

1 You can use Aida or Aida band for this. Measure the depth of your book and double this figure. Add 2.5cm (1in) extra for joining the strip and cut your fabric this length. If using Aida band, check your band is the right width for your design.

2 Find the centre of the band and your chart, and start stitching here. Trim your stitched band to size, fraying the edges on Aida. Iron lightweight interfacing to the back of your work to stiffen the fabric and keep the stitches in place if desired.

3 Place the strip on the book and turn the ends under the front cover. Slipstitch in place.

Bookmarks

These can be made from any stitching fabric including perforated paper.

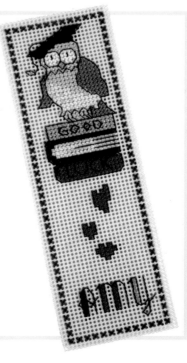

1 Cut your fabric about 15 to 20cm (6 to 8in). Position the top of your design 2.5cm (1in) down from the top of the band. See page 91 if using perforated paper.

2 If using Aida pull out the threads on each side to make a fringe. The rose and lavender bookmark has a much longer fringe at the bottom. Back your bookmark with iron-on interfacing to stiffen it and keep it neat.

Fabric covered albums

The baby albums on pages 8 and 20 were covered with a matching fabric before the tags were attached.

You will need
- Stitched tag
- Matching print fabric
- Photo album
- Double-sided tape and fabric glue

1 Lay the open album out on the fabric. Measure and mark 5cm (2in) from all edges and cut the fabric (see Fig 1). Iron lightweight interfacing to the wrong side.

2 Place the spine of the book in the centre of the fabric and smooth the fabric over the cover. Stick in place with double-sided tape or fabric glue (see Fig 2). Trim most of the surplus fabric above and below the spine, but leave just enough to tuck the edges neatly inside. You may need a little glue to secure this (see Fig 3).

3 Fold the surplus fabric neatly over the edges and stick them to the inside of the covers. Attach two lengths of ribbon, one to each opening edge of the album, for tying in a bow.

4 Cut two pieces of coloured card and fit inside the covers to neaten and finish them. Attach with fabric glue (see Fig 4). Make the tag as explained in stitched tags, step 3 on page 93, and stick it to the cover of your album with fabric glue.

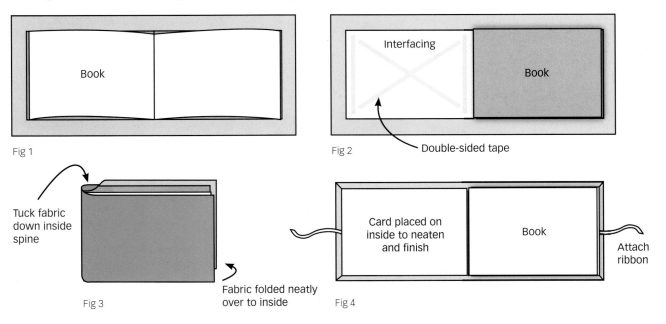

Book

Fig 1

Interfacing

Book

Double-sided tape

Fig 2

Tuck fabric down inside spine

Fabric folded neatly over to inside

Fig 3

Card placed on inside to neaten and finish

Book

Attach ribbon

Fig 4

Bellpulls

Bell pulls like the Mother's Day design on page 62 can be made from strips of fabric, Aida or linen bands.

You will need

- Stitched design
- Broderie anglaise or ribbon
- Bell-pull ends

1 If adding broderie anglaise or another decorative edging, cut your fabric to the size required, allow for turnings and oversew the raw edges. Stitch your design in the centre and fold the surplus fabric to the back. Place the lace at the back with the decorative strip showing at the front, and machine in place.

2 Fold over a 5cm (2in) turning at the top and bottom of the fabric, making sure the raw edges are tucked under. Slipstitch this in place, making sure an opening is left either side of the turning to push the bell-pull end through.

3 Some linen bands like the one on page 62 have eyelets along the edge of the band, through which you can thread matching ribbon. When you reach the end, slipstitch the ribbon in place before turning under the fabric ends.

Drawstring bags

Make your bag to the size required using either Aida or evenweave or a print fabric, and adjust the measurements as required. Add a design to a print fabric using Aida or linen band (see page 91).

1 Cut two pieces of fabric the right size for your bag allowing 2.5cm (1in) extra for seams. Stitch the design directly on to the fabric if using Aida or evenweave. Machine or slipstitch your stitched band or patch in place if using a print fabric.

2 Put the two fabric pieces right sides together and stitch 1.5cm (½in) from the raw edge down the two sides, leaving a 5cm (2in) opening on each side at the top, and along the base of the bag.

3 Trim the bottom corners diagonally. Press the side seams open (you can neaten the edges with zig zag or pinking shears).

4 Turn the top edges over 1.5cm (½in) then 4cm (1½in) to make a hem. Machine stitch 2cm (¾in) from the folded edge and again 2cm (¾in) above to form the casing.

5 Thread a cord or ribbon through the casing. Join the ends together and hide in the casing.

Cakebands

Aida band is ideal for decorating a cake for Easter, Christmas or a child's birthday (see pages 66, 76 and 12).

1 Measure the circumference of the cake and add 2.5cm (1in) for turnings. Fold the band in half and mark the centre with a line of tacking in a contrasting colour. Count the height of your chosen chart and check your Aida band is the right size for this.

2 Calculate how many complete repeats of the pattern you can fit on to your band, finishing at least 4cm (1½in) from either end. Start stitching the design in the centre and work out to each end (see also page 91).

3 Remove the tacking and press the band gently with a cool iron. Iron interfacing to the wrong side to give a firmer finish if preferred. Turn under each end of the band and use sticky tape to keep them together around the cake, or slipstitch them in place.

Other bands

Use the same method descibed for the cakeband to decorate other gifts including towels, napkins, tray cloths or boxes (see pages 68, 76, 82). When the stitching is complete either machine or slipstitch your band in place, remembering to turn under each end to keep it neat.

Fabric cube

Using two different shades of fabric makes this nursery toy even more fun.

You will need
- Six 7.5cm (3in) squares of Aida
- Polyester stuffing

1 Stitch each motif in the centre of a fabric square and iron interfacing to the back.

2 Put the top and bottom squares to one side and sew the other four squares together with right sides touching to form a tube.

3 With right sides together, stitch the top square in position, one seam at a time. Repeat with the bottom square. Leave a gap in the middle of the last seam for stuffing.

4 Fill the cube firmly with polyester stuffing and slipstitch the gap together.

Sachets

You can make sachets from Aida or evenweave fabrics, stitching the design straight on to the fabric, or use a print fabric and sew on a stitched piece as a patch. Gauze or silk fabric is ideal for pot-pourri sachets (see page 81).

Heart sachet template

1 Cut two squares of fabric of your choice allowing 2cm (¾in) for seams. With right sides facing, pin the front and back together.

2 Machine or hand sew the edges leaving a gap on one side. Trim the corners diagonally and turn through.

3 Fill the sachet with wadding or a pot-pourri mixture before slipstitching the seam on the right side.

Heart-shaped sachets

1 The heart-shaped sachets on pages 27 and 83 are made in the same way. Use the template above to cut heart shapes from your fabric, enlarging it on a photocopier if required.

2 Trim the stitched fabric to a smaller heart and slipstitch in place on the sachet. Add beaded rope or ribbon to decorate.

Napkin and napkin ring

It's easy to stitch your own special napkins and matching rings for your festive table from evenweave fabric.

Napkin

1 Hem a 30cm (12in) square of evenweave fabric by folding over 1cm (⅜in) then 1.5cm (½in). Mitre the corners and machine stitch in place.

2 Fold the napkin in half to form a triangle. Use the fold as a centre line and position the centre of the motif 4cm (1½in) from the point of the napkin.

Napkin ring

1 Cut a strip of linen 16.5cm (6½in) long x 5.5cm (2⅛in) wide for each napkin ring. Machine along the edges using a zig-zag stitch or oversew them by hand.

2 Find the centre of both the strip and one of the snowflakes. Start stitching from this point and work outwards. Work three snowflakes.

3 Turn under 5mm (⅛in) at the top and bottom of the strip. Make a turning at each end and iron on some interfacing to keep these in position. Finally, sew on a popper for fastening.

Simple padded door hanger

Wadding is used to pad this fun hanger. It is mounted on card and suspended from matching gingham ties.

You will need
- Stitched piece
- Card, 12.5 x 12.5cm (5 x 5in)
- Gingham fabric
- Double-sided tape or fabric glue

1 Trim the Aida two or three rows away from the design and fringe it all round.

2 Cover the card with wadding cut to the same size. Cut a square of gingham fabric slightly larger than the card and place over the card, turning the edges to the back. Glue or tape these in place making sure the edges and corners are neat.

3 Make the ties from two 38 x 6cm (15 x 2½in) strips of gingham. Fold these in half, length ways, and machine the full length of the strip. Turn them to the right side and turn in the ends and slipstitch together.

4 Place the two lengths of ribbon at the back and secure with tape. Cover this with a smaller square of card to keep the back neat. Place double-sided tape on the back of your stitching and carefully position this on the gingham square. For quickness use 78cm (30in) ribbon, cut in two, for the ties.

Christmas card holder

Use a similar method to make this festive holder from page 76.

1 Cut a square of card the right size and cover with wadding. Place the stitched fabric on top and fold the fabric edges neatly under.

2 Neaten the back and secure the fabric with double-sided tape. Add a ribbon the length and width you require, plus a loop at the top for hanging. I took the ribbon through a brass ring to act as the hanger (see Fig 2). Secure with tape before placing a piece of card cut to size to cover the back (see Fig 3).

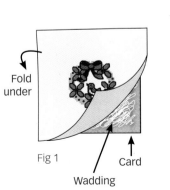

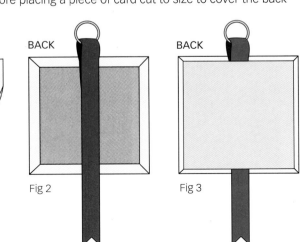

Fold under

Wadding

Card

Fig 1

BACK

Fig 2

BACK

Fig 3

Cutlery wrap

Choose two contrasting print fabrics to make this handy presentation for a cutlery set.

You will need

- Two 20 x 20cm (8 x 8in) squares of contrasting print fabric
- Ribbon
- Button

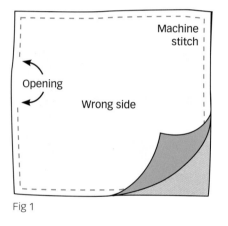

1 Place the fabric pieces with wrong sides together. Pin, tack and machine 5cm (2in) from the edge, leaving an opening at one corner for turning (Fig 1).

2 Turn the fabric to the right side and insert the ribbon to form a loop. Stitch neatly in place. Add a small button on the opposite side so that the ribbon loop will fit snugly over the button (Fig 2), forming a cone to enclose the cutlery set (Fig 3).

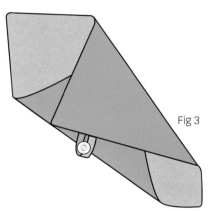

Ribbon

Right side

Fig 2

Button

Machine stitch

Opening

Wrong side

Fig 1

Fig 3

Jam-pot cover

You can also stitch your motif directly on to the gingham fabric using waste canvas as a grid if you prefer.

1 Cut a 23 x 23cm (9 x 9in) square of gingham or another fabric of your choice. Use a bowl or plate as a template and draw a circle in tailor's chalk or pencil.

2 Cut round the circle with pinking shears and then fold the fabric in half and in half again to find the centre. Mark with a pin or some tacking.

3 Trim your stitched design and fringe the edges, leaving one blank square all round to keep your stitches in place. Position in the centre of the fabric and slipstitch in place. Place this fabric over the jam pot and tie with ribbon or string.

Stitched frame

It is a good idea when making a special wedding or graduation frame (see page 30) to ask a professional framer to cut your mount board and assemble your completed frame.

You will need
• Stitched piece
• Frame
• Mount board with aperture
• Pins and fabric scissors
• Double-sided tape

1 Cut your fabric 5cm (2in) larger all round than your mount board and stitch the design in the centre. Back it with iron-on interfacing to prevent the fabric wrinkling.

2 Position the fabric over the mount board and pin along the edges into the board to anchor it. Cut the fabric over the aperture carefully, leaving 5cm (2in) all round the edge. Make diagonal slashes to each corner and turn the surplus fabric to the back. Pin the fabric in place then stick it with double-sided tape.

3 Fold the outer fabric edges to the back and secure these in the same way. Remove the pins and place this mount in your frame

4 insert your photograph behind the stitched mount in its frame.

Christmas stocking

This versatile project means you can easily alter the size of the stocking template below using a photocopier.

You will need
• Stitched stocking design
• Backing fabric
• Ribbon
• Stocking template
• Tailor's chalk

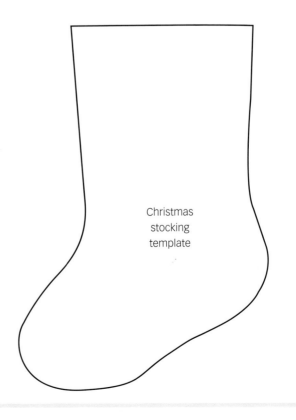

1 Use the stocking template below to cut a paper template, changing the size on a photocopier as required.

2 Carefully position this over the stitched design and draw round it with tailor's chalk and cut out. Draw and cut out a second stocking shape from the fabric. Oversew or zigzag on a machine along the top edges to prevent them from fraying.

3 Place the two pieces right sides together and machine round the stocking, leaving the top open and using a 5cm (2in) seam allowance. Turn the top edges over and slipstitch in place. Add a ribbon loop or tie.

Christmas
stocking
template

Suppliers

UK

Coats Craft
PO Box 22, The Lingfield Estate,
McMullen Road, Darlington,
Co Durham, DL1 1YO
tel: 01325 394 394
www.coatscrafts.co.uk
*For Anchor stranded cotton (floss),
metallic threads and fabrics, and some
Charles Crafts products in the UK.*

Debbie Cripps
8 Christchurch
Street West, Frome,
Somerset BA11 1EQ
tel: 01373 454 448
www.debbiecripps.co.uk
For gift boxes, threads and beads.

DMC Creative World
Pullman Road, Wigston,
Leicester, LE18 2DY
tel: 01162 811 040 for stockists
www.dmc.com
*For baby's bib, padded hanger and soft
toys, DMC stranded cotton (floss) and
Zweigart Aida and linen fabrics.*

Framecraft
Lichfield Road, Brownhills, Walsall,
West Midlands, WS8 6LH
tel: 01543 360 842
www.framecraft.com
*For ready made items that will take
cross stitch inserts including boxes,
coasters, bowls, noteblock holder,
child's ruler and boot clips,
paperweights, pendants, frames, pen
holders, key rings and fridge magnets,
wedding items and credit card holder.*

Sew and So
Stroud House, Russell Street,
Stroud, Glos, GL5 3AN
tel: 0800 013 0150
www.sewandso.co.uk
*For Textile Heritage Aida band, various
colours of perforated paper.*

The American Way
20 Edgbaston Road, Smethwick,
West Midlands, B66 4LQ
tel: 0121 6015454
For Mill Hill perforated paper.

The Viking Loom
22 High Petergate, York, YO1 7EH
tel: 01904 765 599
www.vikingloom.co.uk
For bell pulls and linen band.

Willow Fabrics
95 Town Lane, Mobberly,
Cheshire, WA16 7HH
tel: 0800 056 7811
www.willowfabrics.com
*For linen and Aida fabrics, Aida
and linen bands, beads and threads.*

Wimble Bees
6 City Business Centre
Basin Road, Chichester,
West Sussex, PO19 8DU
tel: 01243 532555
email: sales@wimblebees.com
www.wimblebees.com
For the sipper cup, bibs and caps.

US

Gay Bowles Sales Inc
PO Box 1060
Janesville, WI 53547
tel: (608) 754 9212
fax: (608) 754 0665
For Framecraft products.

Anne Brinkley Designs Inc
3395B Oracle Road,
Tucson, AZ 85705
tel: (520) 888 1462
fax: (520) 888 1483
For Framecraft products.

Crafter's Pride
Daniel Enterprises,
PO Box 685, 2365 Hwy,
210 West Hampstead, NC 28443
www.crafter'spride.com
For the sipper cup.

Charles Craft, Inc
PO Box 1049, Laurenburg, NC 28353
www.charlescraft.com
For baby bibs.

Acknowledgments

Although putting me under pressure at times, this has been an exciting project for me to work on. I love my work and my husband Myke has always been there to support and give encouragement when my confidence has waned. My dear friend Rosemary, your friendship and help has made this book finally come to fruition.

Many people have helped me to achieve this book and I thank them all for their help. For all those at David & Charles, but especially Cheryl Brown for her invaluable advice and encouragement and also Prudence Rogers and Jennifer Proverbs for their patience. Juliet Bracken who edited my text, a great thank you, and Lin Clements for producing such wonderful charts. Hilary at Willow Fabrics who kindly provided a supply of threads, fabric and beads and Maureen at Framecraft for the copious supply of wonderful gifts. Jenny Wilday at DMC for soft toys, fabrics and threads and also Pam at Debbie Cripps for all their help.

None of this book could have been achieved without the expert help of my stitchers, Rosemary Barker, Angela Otterwell and Tina Godwin who have spent many hours of their precious time stitching these designs. Also added thanks to Tina, who gave generously of her time in both making up the gifts and chatting over problems.

About the author

Lesley Teare trained as a textile designer, with a degree in printed and woven textiles. Lesley has been one of DMC's leading designers and her cross stitch designs appear regularly in most needlework magazines including *The World of Cross Stitching* and *Cross Stitcher*. She has contributed designs to three David & Charles titles – *Cross Stitch Greetings Cards*, *Cross Stitch Alphabets* and *Cross Stitch Angels*. Lesley lives in Hitcham, Suffolk.

DMC/Anchor Thread Conversion

The designs in this book use DMC stranded cottons (floss). This DMC/Anchor thread conversion chart is only a guide, as exact colour comparisons cannot always be made. An asterisk * indicates an Anchor shade that has been used more than once so take care to avoid duplication in a design. If you wish to use Madeira threads, telephone for a conversion chart on 01765 640003 or e-mail: acts@madeira.co.uk

DMC	Anchor	DMC	Anchor	DMC	Anchor	DMC	Anchor	DMC	Anchor	DMC	Anchor	DMC	Anchor	DMC	Anchor
B 5200	1	355	1014	604	55	781	308*	912	209	3023	899	3765	170	3846	1090
White	2	356	1013*	605	1094	782	308*	913	204	3024	388*	3766	167	3847	1076*
Ecru	387*	367	216	606	334	783	307	915	1029	3031	905*	3768	779	3848	1074*
150	59	368	214	608	330*	791	178	917	89	3032	898*	3770	1009	3849	1070*
151	73	369	1043	610	889	792	941	918	341	3033	387*	3772	1007	3850	188*
152	969	370	888*	611	898*	793	176*	919	340	3041	871	3773	1008	3851	186*
153	95*	371	887*	612	832	794	175	920	1004	3042	870	3774	778	3852	306*
154	873	372	887*	613	831	796	133	921	1003*	3045	888*	3776	1048*	3853	1003*
155	1030*	400	351	632	936	797	132	922	1003*	3046	887*	3777	1015	3854	313
156	118*	402	1047*	640	393	798	146	924	851	3047	887	3778	1013*	3855	311*
157	120*	407	914	642	392	799	145	926	850	3051	845*	3779	868	3856	347
158	178	413	236*	644	391	800	144	927	849	3052	844	3781	1050	3857	936*
159	120*	414	235*	645	273	801	359	928	274	3053	843	3782	388*	3858	1007
160	175*	415	398	646	8581*	806	169	930	1035	3064	883	3787	904*	3859	914*
161	176	420	374	647	1040	807	168	931	1034	3072	397	3790	904*	3860	379*
162	159*	422	372	648	900	809	130	932	1033	3078	292	3799	236*	3861	378
163	877	433	358	666	46	813	161*	934	852*	3325	129	3801	1098	3862	358*
164	240*	434	310	676	891	814	45	935	861	3326	36	3802	1019*	3863	379*
165	278*	435	365	677	361*	815	44	936	846	3328	1024	3803	69	3864	376
166	280*	436	363	680	901*	816	43	937	268*	3340	329	3804	63*	3865	2*
167	375*	437	362	699	923*	817	13*	938	381	3341	328	3805	62*	3866	926*
168	274*	444	291	700	228	818	23*	939	152*	3345	268*	3806	62*	48	1207
169	849*	445	288	701	227	819	271	943	189	3346	267*	3807	122	51	1220*
208	110	451	233	702	226	820	134	945	881	3347	266*	3808	1068	52	1209*
209	109	452	232	703	238	822	390	946	332	3348	264	3809	1066*	57	1203*
210	108	453	231	704	256*	823	152*	947	330*	3350	77	3810	1066*	61	1218*
211	342	469	267*	712	926	824	164	948	1011	3354	74	3811	1060	62	1202*
221	897*	470	266*	718	88	825	162*	950	4146	3362	263	3812	188	67	1212
223	895	471	265	720	326	826	161*	951	1010	3363	262	3813	875*	69	1218*
224	895	472	253	721	324	827	160	954	203*	3364	261	3814	1074	75	1206*
225	1026	498	1005	722	323*	828	9159	955	203*	3371	382	3815	877*	90	1217*
300	352	500	683	725	305*	829	906	956	40*	3607	87	3816	876*	91	1211
301	1049*	501	878	726	295*	830	277*	957	50	3608	86	3817	875*	92	1215*
304	19	502	877*	727	293	831	277*	958	187	3609	85	3818	923*	93	1210*
307	289	503	876*	729	890	832	907*	959	186	3685	1028	3819	278	94	1216
309	42	504	206*	730	845*	833	874*	961	76*	3687	68	3820	306	95	1209*
310	403	517	162*	731	281*	834	874*	962	75*	3688	75*	3821	305*	99	1204
311	148	518	1039	732	281*	838	1088	963	23*	3689	49	3822	295*	101	1213*
312	979	519	1038	733	280	839	1086	964	185	3705	35*	3823	386	102	1209*
315	1019*	520	862*	734	279	840	1084	966	240	3706	33*	3824	8*	103	1210*
316	1017	522	860	738	361*	841	1082	970	925	3708	31	3825	323*	104	1217*
317	400	523	859	739	366	842	1080	971	316*	3712	1023	3826	1049*	105	1218*
318	235*	524	858	740	316*	844	1041	972	298	3713	1020	3827	311	106	1203*
319	1044*	535	401	741	304	869	375	973	290	3716	25	3828	373	107	1203*
320	215	543	933	742	303	890	218	975	357	3721	896	3829	901*	108	1220*
321	47	550	101*	743	302	891	35*	976	1001	3722	1027	3830	5975	111	1218*
322	978	552	99	744	301	892	33*	977	1002	3726	1018	3831	29	112	1201*
326	59*	553	98	745	300	893	27	986	246	3727	1016	3832	28	113	1210*
327	101*	554	95	746	275	894	26	987	244	3731	76*	3833	31*	114	1213*
333	119	561	212	747	158	895	1044*	988	243	3733	75*	3834	100*	115	1206*
334	977	562	210	754	1012	898	380	989	242	3740	872	3835	98*	121	1210*
335	40*	563	208	758	9575	899	38	991	1076	3743	869	3836	90	122	1215*
336	150	564	206*	760	1022	900	333	992	1072	3746	1030	3837	100*	124	1210*
340	118	580	924	761	1021	902	897*	993	1070	3747	120	3838	177	125	1213*
341	117*	581	281*	762	234	904	258	995	410	3750	1036	3839	176*	126	1209*
347	1025	597	1064	772	259*	905	257	996	433	3752	1032	3840	120*		
349	13*	598	1062	775	128	906	256*	3011	856	3753	1031	3841	159*		
350	11	600	59*	776	24	907	255	3012	855	3755	140	3842	164*		
351	10	601	63*	778	968	909	923*	3013	853	3756	1037	3843	1089*		
352	9	602	57	779	380*	910	230	3021	905*	3760	162*	3844	410*		
353	8*	603	62*	780	309	911	205	3022	8581*	3761	928	3845	1089*		

Index